THE
SETTLERS' WEST

THE SETTLERS' WEST

BY MARTIN F. SCHMITT
AND DEE BROWN

BONANZA BOOKS, NEW YORK

FOR

JOE,

A JACK,

AND A PAIR OF

QUEENS

FOREWORD

THE AMERICAN WEST is many things: exploration and legend, Indians and buffalo, trappers and traders, cowboys and cattle. More enduring than these is the West of the settler—the West of the man who looked for an opportunity on the new land. The frontier was tamed by the home-seeker, the land-hungry, the man who traveled with his family, with seeds and furniture in his wagon box, the man who wrote back to the States "We are in the land of the living, and in the place of hope."

Millions of words in letters, diaries, reminiscences and historical works described the Settlers' West. Few of the words have the power and verity of contemporary photographic records. In this volume the words of the settlers are combined with photographs and illustrations of the same time and place. Here are the faces, the acts, the spirit of the westerner, the settler at work, at play, taming the land, building towns and cities, shaping a way of life. Words and photographs together are as close as anyone may come today to the true nature of the American West.

Settlement of the West began about the time that the photographic process was introduced to America. In 1839, when Frederick Wislizenus, George Catlin and Thomas Jefferson Farnham were traveling their separate ways beyond the Missouri, photography as developed by Louis J. M. Daguerre of France was brought to the United States through the scientific curiosity of Samuel F. B. Morse.

Within a decade the trail of the early explorers and trappers was obscured by the dust of emigrant trains, and daguerreotype crossed the continent. In 1847 Rudolph Friedrich Kurz, Swiss painter, complained at St. Louis, "As artist I had no chance at all . . . daguerreotypists completely crowded out portrait painters." Among Kurz's competitors was J. H. Fitzgibbon who arrived in Missouri in 1846, and captured in daguerreotype the scenes of "Sovereignville" among the border settlements of Missouri, Arkansas and the Cherokee Nation.

In theory, the story of the settlement of the West was within range of photographers from about the time of the Mexican War. The first caravan of western settlers known to photography accompanied the Frederick W. Lander expedition of 1859. With this party along the "Fort Kearney, South Pass and Honey Lake Wagon Road" were Albert Bierstadt of Boston and S. F. Frost of New York, who took "stereopticon views of emigrant trains, Indian camp scenes, etc." Actually, the western scene was not commonly photographed until after the Civil War.

FOREWORD

Of the scarce early daguerreotype records, and later wet-plate and dry-plate photographs of the frontier, many have been lost through fire or careless handling. More than enough have survived, however, to provide a pictorial representation of that social and cultural phenomenon of American history, the Settlers' West.

ACKNOWLEDGMENTS

IT WOULD be impossible to create a book of this nature without the cooperation of persons and institutions who have recognized the importance of photographs, and who have made efforts to collect and preserve prints and negatives. For many libraries and historical societies, the saving of photographic records represents a burden—borne cheerfully by some, grudgingly by others. To those who have saved such records, and who understand the importance of what they have, the authors of this volume owe an incalculable debt.

One of the finest collections in the West is fortunately administered by one of the finest persons, Myrtle D. Berry of the Nebraska State Historical Society. Similar high credit should be given to Virginia Daiker, Prints and Photographs Division, Library of Congress; Opal Harber, Western History Department, Denver Public Library; and Helen M. McFarland, Librarian, Kansas State Historical Society. The greatest of the western collections yet in private hands belongs to Jack E. Haynes of Bozeman, Montana—a fine photographer, a cordial gentleman, and a worthy member of one of the West's most noted photographic families.

Our thanks are due to the following persons who were of great help, either in supplying photographs or information: F. S. Baker, Berkeley, California; Colonel Albert L. Barr, U. S. Air Forces; Ed Bartholomew, Frontier Book Company, Houston, Texas; Richard Chapin, University of Oklahoma; Fog Horn Clancy, New York; Judge Redmond S. Cole, Tulsa, Oklahoma; Mrs. C. E. Cook, Museum Curator, Oklahoma Historical Society; Mrs. J. M. Cornelison, Pendleton, Oregon; R. R. Doubleday, Ponca City, Oklahoma; Malcolm Epley, Jr., Western Pine Association; Art French, University of Oregon; Ruth C. Hamilton, Union Pacific Museum, Omaha; Alvin F. Harlow, New York; Theresa Trost Hartford, Trost Studio, Port Arthur, Texas; William H. Heers, Librarian, U. S. Geological Survey; F. Hal Higgins, Walnut Creek, California; Stewart Holbrook, Portland, Oregon; Lola Homsher, Wyoming State Archivist; George O. Howard, Tulsa, Oklahoma; Icko Iben, University of Illinois; L. H. Jorud, Helena, Montana; Sid Keener, Cooperstown, N. Y.; Dean F. Krakel, Archivist, University of Wyoming; Arthur M. McAnally, Librarian, University of Oklahoma; John McMaster, East St. Louis, Illinois; Alice R. Metzger, Sharlot Hall Historical Museum of Arizona; M. G. Murphy, Lawson Title Company, Beaver, Oklahoma; Margaret. C. Neal, Soil Conservation Service; J. Richard Shaner, American Petroleum Institute; Eleanor B. Sloan, Arizona Pioneers,

ACKNOWLEDGMENTS

Historical Society; George T. Springer, Minneapolis, Minnesota; M. W. Stirling, Director, Bureau of American Ethnology; Robert Talmadge, Library, University of Kansas; John Terrell, Magnolia Petroleum Company; Paul Vanderbilt, Graphic History Society of America; John W. Wagner, Texas Mid-Continent Oil and Gas Association; R. J. Wallace, California Rodeo, Salinas; Earl M. Welty, Union Oil Company of California; Bill M. Woods, University of Illinois.

Institutions of special help were the American Antiquarian Society, California Historical Society, Chicago Historical Society, National Archives and Record Service, and the William R. Coe Collection of Western Americana, Yale University.

The Library of the University of Oregon, Eugene, Oregon, deserves special mention as having one of the greatest collections of western photographs in the country—and for being able to supply demands from the collection.

Grateful acknowledgment is made to the University of Oregon for a grant-in-aid toward the purchase of many of the prints in this volume.

MARTIN F. SCHMITT
DEE BROWN

CONTENTS
AND ILLUSTRATIONS

CONTENTS AND ILLUSTRATIONS

CONTENTS AND ILLUSTRATIONS

CONTENTS AND ILLUSTRATIONS

CONTENTS AND ILLUSTRATIONS

CONTENTS AND ILLUSTRATIONS

CONTENTS AND ILLUSTRATIONS

CONTENTS AND ILLUSTRATIONS

CONTENTS AND ILLUSTRATIONS

CONTENTS AND ILLUSTRATIONS

CONTENTS AND ILLUSTRATIONS

CONTENTS AND ILLUSTRATIONS

CONTENTS AND ILLUSTRATIONS

CONTENTS AND ILLUSTRATIONS

CONTENTS AND ILLUSTRATIONS

THE
SETTLERS' WEST

CHAPTER ONE

WESTWARD MARCH

"Thare is good land on the Massura for a poar mans home."

THIS THEME, penned in an 1838 letter from Arkansas to Tennessee, appears with its variations as the moving spirit of western migration. The frontiersman who scrawled out the good news from the banks of the White River probably had no conception of the wide reach of land between his few acres and the Pacific shore. He dreamed no dreams of empire. His eye was on the good land he had found, where a "poar man" could prosper.

To settlers on the bottom lands of the great mid-western rivers, and on the forested fringes of the great plains, the West of the 1830's was a rumor of indefinite obstacles, mountain and desert, a land populated by savages and near savages. The Spanish country, and the fabled River of the West were names and places for conjecture. The maps of the literate were only a little more useful than the rumors of the semi-literate. The great desert, and the Shining Mountains stood as a barrier to the settlers who had flowed across the Alleghanies.

Beyond the horizon of the settlers were the trappers and traders, less concerned with rumors, correcting the maps while they read them. "The Rocky Mountains," wrote trader Joshua Pilcher in 1830, "are deemed by many to be impassable, and to present the barrier which will arrest the westward march of the American population. The man must know little of the American people who supposes they can be stopped by any thing in the shape of mountains, deserts, seas, or rivers."

That same year the company of Smith, Jackson and Sublette, fur traders, demonstrated that the plains, at least, could be crossed by wagons "in a state of nature." In April, 1830, a caravan of ten wagons and two dearborns left St. Louis and crossed to rendezvous in the Rocky Mountains. Twelve cattle and a milk cow were driven along "for support." Grass was abundant, and buffalo beyond requirements, so that the expedition returned, rich in beaver pelts, with four oxen and the milk cow.

"The wagons," wrote the partners, "could easily have crossed the Rocky Mountains over the Southern Pass." Actually, they agreed, the route from the Pass to the great falls of the Columbia river was easier than the eastern slopes, except for a "scarcity of game."

Two years later, the steamboat *Yellowstone* ascended the Missouri to Fort Pierre on behalf of the American Fur Company, and so demonstrated a second practical means of western travel. The desert was vulnerable by land or water. The way was open for the "poar man" with his family and household goods to find good land "on the Massura"— or beyond.

The settlers came. The Americans were not stopped by any thing. They came, first, for good land; and when gold was discovered the gold-hunters joined the ranks of the land-hungry. First a trickle, then a torrent, the migration westward became a phenomenon in American history unique in numbers and distances. For fifty years the westward migration continued, until the good land from the Missouri to the Pacific was peopled, and the frontier was declared to be past tense.

Crossing the plains and mountains, easy for the professional fur traders and explorers, offered greater obstacles to the land-seekers, amateurs in the business of travel in a tree-less, water-poor wilderness. The emigrants carried more than "twelve cattle and a milk cow." Hunting buffalo was a new experience. The overlanders had not the contempt for difficulties bred by familiarity into the mountain men. The emigrants loaded their goods and families into wagons, and on horseback. Many of them simply walked, pack on back; others pulled handcarts. To all of them the trip was a series of new, strange, and often terrifying incidents.

Many of the first pathbreakers wrote letters home, and prepared itineraries for neighbors and kin who were to follow. "Guides" were published for the aid and comfort of the emigrant. Advice in such literature was based on tragic experience.

"Build strong wagons, with three-inch tires held on by bolts instead of nails."

"Obtain Illinois or Missouri oxen, as they are more adaptable to trail forage, and less likely to be objects of Indian desire."

"Every male person should have at least one rifle gun."

"Of all places in the world, traviling in the mountains is the most apt to breed contentions and quarrils. The only way to keep out of it is to say but little, and mind your own business exclusively."

Whatever the size of outfit, or means of travel, the emigrants shared certain experiences common to all who penetrated the West. Their experiences have become symbols of the trek: the ferries and fords, Chimney Rock, Devil's Gate, the first buffalo, boiling springs, the Pass, alkali deserts, and Indians. The sight of death on the trail was a universal experience—death by cholera, death in childbirth, "mountain fever," or a violent death in battle. The graves, quickly dug and crudely marked, were part of the price paid for the free land, and the great opportunity at the end of the trail.

For those emigrants whose destination was the Pacific coast, and who had more than average means, the sailing ship and steamboat offered a way of reaching the new land without the hardships of the overland route. Many voyagers found, to their sorrow, that they had exchanged one set of hazards for another.

Gradually the major western routes became well defined, the worst gullies were smoothed over, and the steepest grades eased. The Indian threat was subdued. Travel was less hazardous. Toll roads and ferries were established by enterprising persons who tarried on the route, grasping their opportunity on the spot. By the time of the Civil War it was possible to ride an overland stage from Missouri to San Francisco. The stage was comparatively fast, but, as one passenger declared, the ride was "twenty-four days of hell."

Not all western migration was pointed beyond the mountains. The "desert" of the great plains lost much of its terror, and attracted the land-hungry. To the settlers who came from timbered country, the plains were a "perfect ocean of glory." Here one could strike a sod-buster, and circle a section of land without more obstacles than a few buffalo chips. Water was scarce, but the land was good, and a man could always hope.

As the railroads advanced westward with the aid of the land-grant system, settlement of the plains progressed more rapidly, and with a new pattern. The railroad companies recognized the economic importance of population along the right-of-ways. As they laid track, the lines competed for settlers, and offered attractive inducements to prospective emigrants.

In 1885 the Union Pacific posted special rates of forty-five dollars from the Missouri river to Portland, with a free baggage allowance of 150 pounds. Berths in emigrant sleeping cars were free. "The emigrants," said a company leaflet, "are hauled in their own sleeping cars attached to the regular passenger trains."

Agents working for, or in cooperation with, railroad lines sponsored colonies. As Jay Cooke, financier of the Northern Pacific phrased it, "The neighbors in the Fatherland may be neighbors in the new West." To encourage colonists, the Northern Pacific built reception houses, sold "ready-made" homes, offered terms of ten per cent down, and the balance in ten annual payments. The company offered to donate a section of land to each colony for religious purposes.

To the railroad colonies came groups of Civil War veterans looking for a new start, entire congregations from England, and shiploads of emigrants from Europe. Many of the hopeful land-seekers were disappointed in the land, the climate, and in their neighbors, but the stubborn ones endured the first hardships, and subdued the country.

Once a pioneer had arrived at his destination, and taken up his claim, his first concern was for a house. Shelter for his family, rather than architecture was the primary consideration.

The "axe and augur dwelling" was the most common arrangement in a land where timber was easily available. As the name implies, such a house was built of logs, held together by wooden pins and gravity. The result of a workmanlike job was a "snug home in the wilderness." Inept or careless work produced a house "as tight as the end of a woodpile." A mud, stone and sod chimney and fireplace heated the cabin, and provided cooking facilities. The primitive bed, referred to as a "prairie rascal," was the only fixed piece of furniture. Tables and chairs, other than those brought from the east, were rough-hewn. Windows were greased paper or parchment.

On the tree-less plains, the sod-house became a common style of building. With a breaking plough, the settler drove a sixteen-inch furrow through heavy sod. The strip was cut into convenient lengths, and the sections laid like brick. Rafters, covered with hay and then with sod, provided a roof. Some of the prairie homes were neat, others simply holes in the ground. Well made, they were comfortable; ill made, they drove the pioneer housewife mad.

As a settler prospered, he built a home more closely resembling the one he might have left behind. Sawmills were established, and lumber made available. The log house, and soddy gradually vanished, and the frame house with a shake roof took its place. The wealthy imported ideas and habits from the east, hired labor skilled with a scroll saw, and built stately mansions with crusty decorations, a style known as "steamboat gothic."

Once the West was conquered by trail, rail and road, memories of the early-day adventures, hardships, and privations began to assume the qualities of a romance. The "pioneer" appeared as a special type, imbued with the spirit of Manifest Destiny, the major character of a national saga, rather than a man of average quality in search of more and better land. Pioneer societies were formed among the "first comers."

Some of the longer-lived and more vocal emigrants devoted much time and effort to recollecting the picturesque past. Such an one was Ezra Meeker, who crossed the plains in 1852. Meeker, prototype of the far West's "oldest inhabitant," spent his latter years retracing the Oregon Trail.

Encouraged by a sympathetic public, and assisted by the sale of post cards depicting himself, Ezra set his trail eastward in 1906, with a covered wagon, and a team of steers. He called his trip "the Oregon Trail Monument Expedition." His adventures on the road back included a running battle with souvenir hunters, who hacked at his wagon, signed their names on the canvas, and pulled hairs from the tails of his steers. The old pioneer finally reached Washington, D. C., where he shook hands with the cowboy in the White House, Teddy Roosevelt. Meeker did much to stimulate popular interest in the history of overland migration, and the "Oregon Trail" cult dates from his efforts.

In contrast to Meeker was the opinion of Sallie Long, pioneer daughter, who referred to the societies of emigrants as "pioneer imbeciles," and prophesied that "If the public and private words and deeds of most of them were all published, it would prove a record alike discreditable to them and their descendants."

Somewhere between the uncritical enthusiasm of Meeker and the irritation of Sallie Long stands the veritable Westerner, the pioneer, the "poar man who looked for good land on the Massura." "I have always lived in the West," said Ed Howe, "and the many pioneers I have known seemed to feel they were better off than they had been before."

In these chapters are the faces of the western pioneer, from the days when the trail over desert and mountain was first cut by wagon wheels, to the coming of the railroad, and the time when the frontier became folklore. Here is the Westerner at work, at play, building his civilization to conform to his environment, practicing his religion, devising his politics; a man subduing the wilderness.

THE AMERICAN WEST

The American West of the early eighteen-hundreds was a land of rumor, known in its parts by a few trappers and explorers, known as a whole by no one. The sources of its great rivers, the extent of its mountain ranges were a matter of vague conjecture by geographers, who often depicted the continental features as they "must be" rather than as they were.

MOUNTAIN BARRIER

To the westward-pushing settlers, the land beyond the Missouri was barricaded by mountains that could not be crossed by wagons, the Shining Mountains, eternally snow-covered.

THE GREAT PLAINS

Even the approaches to the mountains were forbidding. Between the western edge of settlement and the Great Divide lay the tree-less plains, where wind and alkali dust accompanied fierce storms. Here tribes of savage Indians roamed the prairie in search of buffalo. It was not a place to find a new home.

TO THE ROCKIES BY WAGON

In 1830, a company of fur traders demonstrated that the plains and mountains of the West could be traversed by wagons "in a state of nature." Ten wagons, and two dearborns crossed from St. Louis to rendezvous in the Rocky Mountains. With the wagons went twelve cattle and a milk cow. All the wagons, four cattle, and the milk cow returned. The conquest of the West by settlers was possible. The westward March of the American people could not be stopped by any thing.

CIRCULAR.

TO THE OREGON EMIGRANTS.

Gentlemen:

It being made my duty, as Superintendent of Indian affairs, by an Act passed by the Legislature of Oregon, "to give such instructions and directions to Emigrants to this Territory, in regard to their conduct towards the natives, by the observance of which, they will be most likely to maintain and promote peace and friendship between them and the Indian tribes through which they may pass," allow me to say in the first place, that the Indians on the old road to this country, are friendly to the whites. They should be treated with kindness on all occasions. As Indians are inclined to steal, keep them out of your camps. If one or two are admitted, watch them closely. Notwithstanding the Indians are friendly, it is best to keep in good sized companies while passing through their country. Small parties of two or three are sometimes stripped of their property while on their way to this Territory, perhaps because a preceding party promised to pay the Indians for something had of them, and failed to fulfil their promise. This will show you the necessity of keeping your word with them in all cases.

There is another subject upon which I would say a few words. A number of the emigrants of 1845 took a cut off, as it is called, to shorten the route, leaving the old road; the consequence was, they were later getting in, lost their property, and many lost their lives. Some of those who reached the settlements, were so broken down by sickness, that it was some months before they recovered sufficient strength to labor.

A portion of the emigrants of 1846 took a new route, called the southern route. This proved very disastrous to all those who took it. Some of the emigrants that kept on the old road, reached this place as early as the 13th of September, with their wagons, and all got in, in good season, with their wagons and property, I believe, except a few of the last party. While those that took the southern route, were very late in reaching the settlements—they all lost more or less of their property—many of them losing all they had and barely getting in with their lives; a few families were obliged to winter in the Umpqua mountains, not being able to reach the settlements.

I would therefore recommend you to keep the old road. A better way may be found, but it is not best for men with wagons and families to try the experiment.

My remarks are brief, but I hope may prove beneficial to you.

Dated at Oregon City, this 22d of April, 1847.

GEO. ABERNETHY,

Governor of Oregon Territory and
Superintendent of Indian Affairs.

FREE LAND, FAIR PROSPECTS

To the poor man in search of a better home, the wilderness that was the Oregon Country invited. Traversed by Lewis and Clark, stronghold of the Hudson's Bay Company, and enthusiastically described by missionaries, the Willamette Valley drew settlers two thousand miles over desert, mountain, and plain. The Territorial Governor advised emigrants on choice of routes, and trail conduct.

SWEET BETSY FROM PIKE

The average emigrant was not wealthy. By contemporary account, "His tone was dim, not to say subdued. His clothes butternut. His boots enormous piles of rusty leather, red from long travel, want and woe. From a corner of his mouth trickled 'ambeer.' His old woman, riding in the wagon, smoked a corn-cob pipe, and distributed fragments of conversation all around." So many of them seemed to come from the Pike country in Missouri that the place achieved lasting fame in an overland ballad. The group above gathered for a photograph at the summit of South Pass.

WAGONS WEST (on facing page, top)

For their "journey o'er the plains" most westerners found a canvas-covered wagon the best vehicle. Wide tires kept the wheels from sinking into the sand. Illinois or Missouri oxen, most quickly adapted to trail forage, hauled the loads. During the travel season, May to September, lines of these prairie schooners stretched from the Missouri to the Snake rivers.

NIGHT CORRAL (on facing page, bottom)

Trail customs became standardized by experience and force of circumstance. Every well-run wagon train formed a corral of vehicles at the end of the day's journey for protection against Indians, and to provide a fenced inclosure for livestock. The Fisk Expedition crossed from Minnesota to Montana in 1866.

THE FORD

All western rivers could be forded at some point. At an easy crossing, the stream was shallow, and the ox teams simply pulled the wagons through. At deeper crossings, oxen and cattle had to swim; the wagons were converted into crude boats. Accidents at fords were common, and many an emigrant ended his journey swept down the river.

TWO WHEELS, ONE OX (on facing page, top)

For settlers with no baggage or little money, the luxury of a prairie schooner was abandoned in favor of carts. Other emigrants walked across the plains with packs on back. The Mormon handcart migration between 1856 and 1860 was propelled by man-power. There were instances of persons starting the journey pushing wheelbarrows.

CROSSING THE KAW (on facing page, bottom)

As the western emigrant trails became established, enterprising persons rigged ferries across the larger streams along the route. Such ferries were usually the cable and scow type, motivated by the river current. Ferry proprietors were necessarily rough characters, they had to defend their business from competitors, and persons offering shotgun toll. This ferry crossed the Kaw river.

CANYON PASSAGE

Mountain trails, as well as river crossings, were an impediment to western travel. Space between the water's edge and canyon walls was sometimes barely enough for wagon wheels. When the cliffs pressed too closely, wagons waded to the other side, or used the stream bed as a road. At one point on the Mullan Road, regarded as an improved route, the St. Regis river had to be crossed nineteen times in six miles. The emigrants *(above)* are descending Echo Canyon to the Salt Lake valley.

THE CROOKED STRAIGHT, ROUGH PLACES PLAIN

Mountain travel was made easier when toll roads were established. Road builders constructed easier grades, kept the road free from fallen trees, and filled in the worst holes. Dollarhide's Station *(above)* on the toll road across the Siskiyou mountains from California to Oregon, was a major travel point. Through these gates passed stage coaches, freight wagons, circus trains, pack mules, gold hunters, itinerant preachers, and travellers whose business was best not asked. It was a lively spot to be.

MISSOURI STEAMBOAT

Much of the hardship associated with overland travel could be avoided by taking passage on a Missouri river steamboat to Fort Benton, head of navigation. While steamboat travel upstream was slower than a brisk walk, it was also more comfortable, and usually safer. Though most important as carriers of freight, steamboats brought many emigrants on the first leg of their trip to a new land. The *F. Y. Batchelor* of the Fort Benton Packet Company nudges an upriver landing *(above)*.

SAN FRANCISCO HARBOR, 1851

For western travellers with money, sailing or steaming around the Horn, or via the Isthmus to the Pacific coast was a way of escaping alkali dust. During the California gold rush, passengers and crew alike abandoned ship in San Francisco harbor to seek their fortunes. Ships were anchored helplessly until repentant sailors, disappointed in the diggings, came back to work. Passage on 'Frisco-bound vessels was less hazardous than overland trips, but scurvy, storm, starvation, and lack of water took their toll.

TRAIL TOLL

On land or sea, death visited the emigrants. Most frequent was death by cholera. Little time was spent by travellers in mourning or burying. Rude markers or none at all were placed above the graves. Among the headstones which survived was that of George Winslow. On May 13, 1849, Winslow chided his wife in a letter, "I see that you have the blues a little in your anxiety for my welfare. I do not worry about myself, then why should you for me. Let us for the future look on the bright side of the subject." On June 8, Winslow was dead, his grave marked better than most, with a hastily carved stone.

TRAIL GUARD

Indians, too, were a hazard of the overland trail. "As long as I live," warned Red Cloud of the Sioux, "I will fight you for the last hunting grounds of my people." The United States Army garrisoned the plains routes, but the few soldiers could not protect every dangerous mile of the road. *(Above,* Ft. Rice, Dakota Territory, 1865).

TWENTY-FOUR DAYS OF HELL

Stage travel overland, possible by 1858, was better than walking. One passenger's verdict was abrupt, "I know what hell is; I just had twenty-four days of it." The stagecoach had its own hazards, as recorded in an epitaph mentioned by Bishop Talbot:

> Weep, stranger, for a father spilled
> From a stagecoach, and thereby killed;
> His name, Jay Sykes, a maker of sassengers,
> Slain with three other outside passengers.

The overland stage (*above*) is leaving Virginia City, Montana.

PRAIRIE MOTOR

Efforts to improve means of overland travel led to some odd innovations. At about the same time, 1859 and 1860, Joseph Renshaw Brown of Minnesota and Thomas L. Fortune of Mount Pleasant, Kansas, conceived the idea of a steam-propelled wagon, a Prairie Motor, designed to haul freight over the plains. Both the Fortune wagon *(above)* and Brown's device proved impractical for freight work. They were advised to hitch their wagons to a plough.

THE LAST SPIKE

Final conquest of the western plains and mountains was made by the railroads. In 1869 the Union Pacific celebrated its meeting with Central Pacific at Promontory Point, Utah. On September 8, 1883 the Northern Pacific had its "last spike" ceremony between Garrison and Gold Creek, Montana. Present at the celebration was Henry Villard. The Crow Indians held solemn council on the spot *(above)* and decided the iron horse was come to stay.

2,000,000 FARMS of Fertile Prairie Lands to be had Free of Cost

IN

CENTRAL DAKOTA

The United States offers as a Gift Two Million Farms to Two Million Families who will occupy and improve them. These Lands lie between the 44th and 46th degrees of latitude, and between Minnesota and the Missouri River. In this belt is about

30 Millions OF Acres

Of the Most Productive Grain Lands in the World. The attached Map shows the Location of these Lands.

THIS MAP SHOWS THE ROUTE of the MINNESOTA AND DAKOTA BRANCHES OF THE **Chicago & North-Western R'y** AND OF ITS Winona & St. Peter, Chicago & Dakota, and Dakota Central Branches, INTO THE "FREE" LAND DISTRICT OF CENTRAL DAKOTA

DISTANCES.

Chicago to Winona, Minn.	287 Miles
Chicago to Tracy, Minn.	335
Chicago to Watertown, Dak.	625
Chicago to Volga, Dak., on Sioux River,	605
Chicago to Huron, Dak., on Dakota River,	670
Tracy to Volga, on Sioux River,	70
Sioux River, at Volga, to Huron, on Dakota River,	65
Huron to Missouri River,	120
Missouri River to Deadwood, about	130
Chicago to Missouri River, near Fort Pierre,	790

YOU NEED A FARM!

Here is one you can get simply by occupying it. It will be noticed that the

CHICAGO AND NORTH WESTERN

Has Two Lines of Road that run through to these Lands. It is the only Rail Road that reaches them.

In the Districts to the West, North and South of Watertown, are many millions of acres that you can reach by the CHICAGO & NORTH-WESTERN RAILWAY. Along its Line in Dakota have been laid out a number of Towns in which are needed the Merchant, Mechanic and Laborer.

CENTRAL DAKOTA is now, for the first time, open to settlement. The Indians have been removed and their reservations offered to those who wish to occupy them.

HOW TO GET THERE

Any Ticket Agent should be able to sell you Tickets via the CHICAGO & NORTH-WESTERN RAILWAY, to TRACY or MARSHALL, Minnesota, or to WATERTOWN, Dakota. At Tracy you can get Tickets to all Stations West on the Line in Dakota. From Watertown, or from any Stations West of Marshall, you can get conveyances that will take you to the Lands West, North or South of the Lake Kampeska Line of the Railroad. All Agents of the CHICAGO & NORTH-WESTERN RAILWAY can sell you Tickets to these Lands.

AT CHICAGO YOU CAN BUY TICKETS AT

62 CLARK STREET; 75 CANAL STREET, Corner of Madison; at the WELLS STREET DEPOT, on Kinzie Street, north of Wells Street Bridge; and at KINZIE STREET DEPOT, on the Corner of Kinzie and Canal Streets.

BEAR IN MIND You can not get to the Lands by Rail Road, unless you go via the

Chicago & North-Western R'y.

John Anderson & Co., Printers, Chicago.

TWO MILLION FARMS

Passage of the Union Pacific Land Grant Act in 1862 assured the rapid settlement of the western great plains. Railroad companies realized that right-of-way population meant income from otherwise useless property. They set about gathering and locating settlers. "2,000,000 farms of fertile prairie lands to be had free of cost" was the urgent call of the Chicago and North Western Railway.

COLONISTS

To settle the vast prairie lands, railroad immigration agents sought out entire congregations and villages. "The neighbors in the fatherland may be neighbors in the new West," said Jay Cooke. The Northern Pacific built reception houses for the trainloads of new settlers at Glyndon, Minnesota *(above)*, Yeovil, Detroit Lakes, and other emigration centers.

RUSSIAN EMIGRANTS AT BISMARCK

To the tree-less plains came families from Russia. To them, the scenes of North Dakota looked familiarly like the steppes of their native land.

DUNKERS FROM INDIANA

Max Bass, remarkable promotion agent of the Great Northern Railroad, gathered a colony of Dunkers from Indiana, and settled them in North Dakota. The special train made up to transport the colony was routed through Indiana, Illinois and Wisconsin by daylight, so the public could read the banners hung on the cars. "From Indiana to the Rich, Free Lands in North Dakota, the Bread Basket of America!" The train stopped in the Union Station at St. Paul, where Max Bass arranged to have a photograph taken *(above)*. On March 3, 1894, the Dunkers arrived at Cando, and began a new life as wheat farmers.

RANCH HOUSE

The ranch-type home, a one-story, flat-roofed, rambling structure, flourished in country where there was little rain or snow. It was essentially an imitation of the successful adobe of the southwest. Boggs' Ranch on the Purgatory river, southern Colorado (*above*) was located and built by Thomas O. Boggs in 1867. Here Kit Carson spent his last days.

HOME IN THE WILDERNESS (*on facing page, top*)

Whether on a wheat ranch, in the gold fields, or on an Oregon donation land claim, the first consideration of the pioneer was shelter. In timbered country, the log house was the common type. Not everyone could afford such a house; there were settlements where log-house dwellers were considered "tony," while their more democratic neighbors existed in dugouts and tents. This Iowa log house of the 1850's was referred to as "tight as the end of a woodpile."

SOD SHANTY ON THE PLAINS (*on facing page, bottom*)

Beyond the tree belt, sod formed the basic ingredient of building. Eighteen-inch strips were cut into suitable lengths and laid like bricks. The floors were pounded earth, the windows oiled paper or glass, depending on finances and personal preferences. To the sod house of western Nebraska with its dirt roof and shored-up walls the rancher brought his bride; here he raised his family.

TRAILER HOUSE

A home on wheels was most convenient for Isaac Baker, photographer in the California gold fields, 1853. Gypsy-fashion, the daguerreotype artist travelled from one settlement and mining community to another. Batchelder's Daguerrian Saloon *(above)* was more comfortable and adequate than many of the tents and log shanties erected by the miners. Photographer Baker found better diggings in "likenesses" than in the mines.

.OLD MORMON HOUS

MORMON MULTIPLEX

The Latter Day Saints, creators of many western monuments, were especially remarkable from an architectural point of view. Their Temple and Tabernacle are noteworthy in the annals of western building. In his multiple dwelling *(above)* a Saint could live in peace with his wives and family.

POVERTY

When Ephraim Swain Finch arrived in western Nebraska in the 1880's, he built his family a log-and-mud house. This was better than the common soddy favored by many of his neighbors. Finch prospered. Twenty years later he was able to boast a house of seasoned

AND PROGRESS

lumber, with scroll-saw decorations. The two homes of "Uncle Swain" *(above)* tell a story of pioneer architecture from the frontier period to the first days of prosperity.

LITTLE GRAY HOME IN THE WEST

The interior of a prosperous frontiersman's home offered opportunity for refinement, and display of taste. The G. S. Barnes home at Fargo, North Dakota *(above)*, was noted in 1883 for its quantity of Victorian decoration, imported art work, and for its inclusion of every elegant detail. The Barnes family, bankers, had come as far as possible from the "prairie rascal" string bed of the frontier log house, from the one-room, all-purpose soddy that served the emigrant family. Here was splendor on the western frontier.

LOOKING BACKWARD

As the western pioneer aged and prospered, he reminisced in a romantic spirit. The story of his adventures became a saga. Some of the longer-lived pioneers devoted much of their time to recalling the nobler aspects of the past. Ezra Meeker (*above*), overlander of 1852, was such a man. He dramatized his recollections by driving an ox team east in 1906 along the Oregon Trail.

THE COPYRIGHTED WESTERNER

Ezra Meeker's efforts appealed to the romantic heart of America, and the story of the winning of the West became a popular theme for poetry, drama, and fiction. Western ways were adopted by westerners who never before realized the obligation. The ideal of the pioneer was attached to commercial ventures, and the covered wagon hid a multitude of promotional sins. The "western" movie and the fictional western developed a formula of the great plains as seen from a car window, not on the West as it looked from the papered windows of a sod house.

CHAPTER TWO

THE BIG ROLLING LAND

Come to the Garden of the West! Come to Kansas! Come to Minne-sota! Come to Nebraska, the Great Platte Valley. Soldiers Entitled to a Homestead of 160 Acres. Purchasers, their wives and children car-ried free in our elegant day coaches. Red River Valley Lands. Home-seekers! A Farm for $3 per Acre! Every Farmer, Every Farmer's Son, Every Clerk, Every Mechanic, Every Laboring Man Can Secure a Home.

THE RICH romantic place names of the big rolling land beyond the Mississippi echoed across the eastern United States. Broadsides in all the languages of Europe made the strange Indian names of the faraway country familiar to emigrants long before they reached New York en route to the free lands extending to the Shining Mountains and the Pacific. The slow march of settlement which had followed the Homestead Act of 1862 turned into a stampede during the 1870's and 1880's.

Thousands of human beings moved out upon the great empty plains into an awe-some surreal world of limitless earth and sky. For some it was a world of beauty and freedom, for others it was frightening, sometimes maddening in its loneliness.

The young farming men and their women and children came from everywhere. Their first days were hard, but a few like John Ruede from Pennsylvania found time to scrawl letters to the folks back home: "Staked two corners of my claim this morning. . . . Looking for a place to make our dugout." Two days later Ruede recorded: "We got through digging the hole by the time it was dark. The hole is 10 x 14 feet, and in front 4 ft. deep, 4½ behind. On Monday we must look for a ridge pole and dig steps so we can get into the place."

Within the week, sod walls twenty inches thick were up above the ground, and Ruede wrote on Saturday—just nine days after staking his claim: "Used part of the straw on the roof, and covered the whole roof with a layer of sod, and then threw dirt on it, and the 'House' was finished."

Next day, Ruede was planting gooseberry bushes along the west side of his sod-house and making arrangements for help with his well-digging and sod-breaking.

The new settlers used different words to explain why they moved west, but beyond all their words was the old American vision of a better life beyond the far horizon. "We wanted to come to a new country," said Susan Frances Lomax, "so our children could grow up with the country. We were living on a good farm [in Mississippi]. My husband said he would live ten years longer by coming to a new country. You hardly ever saw a gray headed man. I did not want to come to Texas at all; I dreaded the Indians in those days. . . . It was a hard time on weman; they staid at home and did the work while the men were on their ponies hunting or looking after stock."

Without their yoked oxen, thousands of homesteading families could never have plowed their first fields or hauled wood and water. And in the dark days of the settlers' first blizzardy winters, more often than not it was the dependable ox that was sacrificed for food to keep them alive until spring.

Patient, plodding, stolid—never romantic. That was the ox, an animal neglected both by poets and historians. Rarely does this beast of burden appear in western fiction or motion pictures. Alongside the graceful galloping horse, the colorless castrated ox does not shine in the saga of the West.

Oxen, however, were usually considered as members of the family, endowed by their owners with affectionate or dignified names. A Texan called his pair Pollux and Castor, and in a letter to a friend back in Ohio he wrote: "I have wished a hundred times that they had broke their necks the time that they run away. They however have got to behave themselves and I have gave them Christian names, Dick Polax and Dimann Castor."

Everything but land and sky was scarce on the early western homesteads. Water was usually the scarcest necessity of all. As soon as a settler marked his claim and set up a wagon-cover tent, he started searching for water. The nearest stream might be ten miles away, and water had to be hauled in barrels until a well could be dug. One Nebraska farmer hauled water two years before he could complete digging his well by hand. He dug three hundred feet straight down through hard clay and rock with a pick and shovel.

Edward E. Dale, reminiscing of early days in Oklahoma, recalled asking a farmer why he persisted in hauling water nine miles for his horse and livestock, instead of digging a well. Replied the farmer: "It's just as near to water one way or the other, and I prefer to get mine along horizontal rather than perpendicular lines."

Itinerant well-drillers finally solved the water problem for most western settlers. The usual charge was twenty cents per foot for a hole six inches in diameter, the owner to furnish the necessary iron casing.

Water was pulled out of the deep wells with windmills, and the first homesteaders built huge ones, assuming that the bigger the wheels the more water would flow. In some areas, Dutch-type windmills were built and used for milling grain as well as for pumping water. "Jumbo" windmills were popular, requiring no tower, being merely a large fan-wheel in a crude box. Travelers were impressed by one early ranch on the plains which had a "double-header windmill with two power wheels twenty-two feet in diameter seventy-two feet from the ground."

Finding fuel for cooking and heating was often another major problem for the plains settlers. In the southwest, the pioneers dug mesquite sprouts from the dry earth; in other sections the best woodlands were often on Indian reservations, and the Indians collected a fee—about fifty cents a load—for firewood cut by the homesteaders.

During the first decade of settlement following the Civil War, buffalo chips were the surest and most common source of fuel. Gathered into wagons, carts, or wheelbarrows, the chips were stacked in ricks or piled under a shed to insure dryness; they would not burn when wet.

Later, along the great cattle trails, cow chips replaced the vanishing buffalo dung. But as late as 1880, buffalo chips were still in good supply in some parts of Kansas. The Kinsley *Graphic* carried the following notice on January 17 of that year: "The County Commissioners at their last meeting issued an order to the township trustees that they would allow no bills for coal for the poor, in cases where the poor have teams to gather buffalo chips."

When the buffalo and cow chips, the mesquite roots, and the few trees along the streams were all gone, the plains settlers learned how to burn sunflowers and hay—both in plentiful supply. The sunflower advocates claimed one acre would produce twelve cords of fuel, but unfortunately the twelve cords burned faster than one cord of wood.

Hay burned even faster, and in spite of several ingenious hay-burner stoves developed during the 1880's, a common saying of the times was that it required "two men and a boy to keep a hay fire going." One of the more successful hay burners consisted of several metal cylinders half the length of the firebox and open at one end. Inside each cylinder was a coiled spring attached to the closed end. The walls of the cylinder near the open end were pierced by a number of small holes. The spring was pushed down by packing the cylinder tightly with hay, which was then lighted at one of the holes. As the fuel burned, the spring pressed a fresh supply into the fire, and empty cylinders were replaced with freshly filled ones. Such a stove required constant attention, especially on a cold winter night.

Few of the early western homesteaders could afford even the crude farm machinery of that time. Many a first crop was put in with hoes, spades, and mattocks. Because corn was grown on almost every farm, one of the first "machines" acquired was either a foot or hand corn planter. "This labor saving device," read one advertisement for the hand planter, "is important to the farmers of the West. It is carried or used like a walking stick or cane. It is simple, cheap, accurate, and dependable."

Slightly more complex was the foot planter: "This small, neat corn-planter is buckled on the foot. The operator carries the corn for planting in a small bag. The planter is connected to this bag by an elastic tube through which the seed corn is conveyed. When the foot is raised to make a step, a grain of corn drops into a chamber in the planter. When the foot comes down on the ground, the corn is pressed into the earth."

As the settlers prospered, they began buying newly invented machines. Across the expanding wheat country during the 1870's, reapers and binders and harvesters appeared in a variety of types and models. Unaccustomed to anything more complicated than a plow, the horses did not always cooperate. In his diary, a western farmer proudly noted the acquisition of a stalk-cutting machine, then a few days later laconically recorded: "Finished cutting stalks. The horses ran away and broke stalk-cutter all to hell."

But as early as 1878, the Dickinson County (Kansas) *Chronicle* reported that a young lady of the community was successfully operating a farm with machines: "She does her own plowing—using a sulky plow. This year she has one hundred acres of fine wheat and will cut and bind it herself—using a self-binder."

Newcomers to the West soon discovered that they had less to fear from the highly publicized "savage Indians" than from the violence of Nature—especially the capricious weather which could be more deadly destructive than a war party of savage braves.

The most common enemy was the prairie fire, a particularly awesome spectacle after nightfall. Prairie grass grew as high as a man's head, and during rainless autumns it dried and browned under the sun until it was more inflammable than pitchpine.

"A ribbon of smoke in the distance," wrote Wiley Britton, "it rapidly increased in size, and in a very short time became a great volume of dense black smoke, with tongues of flame shooting high into the air, and a few minutes later we saw hawks and birds of the prairies flying wildly before the sea of surging, writhing and leaping flames. In an incredibly short time the whole visible horizon to the southwest was darkened by the thick black smoke, ashes and flames, and then came antelope, deer, jack rabbits and wolves, racing with the roaring, billowy, writhing flames, in mad flight for safety."

Until settlers learned to plow fire breaks around their fields and cabins, the only methods of defense were to set backfires, beat out the flames with brush, or run a drag over the line of fire. Drags were often hastily improvised, as was Teddy Roosevelt's when he stopped a fire threatening his Dakota ranch by splitting a steer in half and dragging it across the flames.

Twentieth century westerners may believe they have bigger wind and dust storms than the pioneer settlers, but early accounts of the plains country belie these modern claims. One old story of a Kansas cowtown tells of a barber who while shaving a customer chanced to glance out the window and see his first dust storm, a solid wall of blackness descending upon the town. "God almighty!" cried the barber, "the end of the world has come. I'm headin' for home to be with my family." He ran out into the street, leaving his customer to meet doom with a lathered face.

The winds were as awesome as the dust they carried before them. The Wichita *Eagle* in 1872 reported winds lifting "ten-pound boulders and two-year-old mule colts off the ground—the squawking flock overhead may be geese, may be jackasses. Those of us who have lost their domestic animals and fowls need not be alarmed, as the chances are that such stock will be blown back by the next wind."

With its fearful roar and death-dealing funnel, the tornado was a terror to lonely plains dwellers. As a defense against this monster, the settlers built storm cellars. They soon learned to make jokes and tell tall tales about twisters and the huge hail stones which usually accompanied them. "The twisting motion of the wind," a newspaper reported, "drew all the milk from one farmer's herd of cows and sprayed it into the air where it became mixed with small pellets of hail and made a veritable downfall of ice cream. Some pretty big hail fell. One chunk will furnish ice to the meat shops for the next 90 days. Another imbedded itself in the ground and is slowly melting, will afford water to stock all summer and also make a fine boating pond."

Blizzard and flood tales of the West are legion, and many of them are tragic. Both these weather phenomena often came suddenly, the blizzards blowing up late on a hazy warm day, and the floods rushing down dry runs where water was seldom seen. Inexperienced homesteaders were sometimes caught away from home by blizzards, unaware until too late of how rapidly the temperature could drop and of how low was the visibility in a howling snowstorm on the plains.

Not all were so lucky as the Colorado rancher lost in a driving blizzard. Encountering a buffalo floundering around in a deep drift, the rancher quickly slew and disemboweled the animal, then crawled inside, drawing the opening tight to keep out the cold. Next morning when he awoke the rancher found his exit hole frozen shut. He solved his double problem of imprisonment and hunger by eating his way out.

Stories of Nature's violence in the west gradually drifted back to the east, reviving old tales of the Great American Desert. To counteract these stories, Henry Worrall of Topeka drew a charcoal sketch, "Drouthy Kansas," depicting huge corn stalks, grapes, watermelons, and potatoes. Worrall's caricature was reprinted all over the country, and tall tales about Kansas soon became the fashion.

In 1884 some eastern newspapers carried a story of a Kansas farmer who climbed to the top of a cornstalk one evening to inspect the state of the weather. His foot slipped and he fell into a nearby tree top where he dangled precariously by his suspenders all night. When he was rescued the next morning he swore he would buy an almanac and keep himself posted on the weather without resorting to such dangerous methods as climbing tall cornstalks. The Kiowa *Herald* of July 8, 1885, commented on this story: "Coming from an eastern paper, we don't believe it. If he had fallen out of the top of a cornstalk in a field of Barber County corn the blades would have been so thick and strong that they would have sustained his weight and he could reach the ground as easily as walking down a step ladder, and not been put to the painful necessity of hanging all night in a tree top with only his suspenders between him and eternity."

In the summer of 1874, before flying saucers were invented, farmers all over the West began seeing strange silvery spots circling in the sunny skies. The puzzled plainsmen soon discovered what the silvery circles were—millions of grasshoppers in flight. Before that summer ended, 1874 was known as the Great Grasshopper Year.

From Oregon to the Dakotas, south to Texas and east into Missouri, the insects descended upon the land in columns 150 miles wide and 100 miles long, beating like hail against the roofs and sides of farmhouses. Tormented homesteaders tied strings around their trousers bottoms to keep the pests from crawling up and biting their legs. At Fort Scott, Kansas, a descending grasshopper cloud stopped a horse race, covering the tracks three inches deep. Lighting upon trees, they broke limbs under their weight.

Efforts to save crops were futile. Hundred-acre cornfields vanished in a few hours, the plants denuded to the stalks. When blankets and sheets were spread over precious vegetable patches, the grasshoppers ate the bed clothing. One account tells of a man who lay down to rest beside a road; when he awoke his throat and wrists were bleeding from the bites of starving grasshoppers. They ate harness, window curtains, hoe handles, and even each other.

When a dark cloud of grasshoppers landed upon the Union Pacific tracks near Kearney, Nebraska, they stopped all trains, grease from the crushed insects setting locomotive wheels to spinning.

News of this major victory for the grasshoppers came as an anticlimax. Many Great Plains farmers had already given up, and wagon after wagon filled with household goods moved eastward with "Grasshopper" signs on their sides, like the Pike's Peak "Busters" of an earlier decade.

One group of disillusioned settlers, returning through Topeka, stopped there long enough to speak their minds to Henry Worrall of "Drouthy Kansas" fame. "Had it not been for the diabolical seductiveness of that picture," reported the Topeka *Commonwealth*, "they said they would never have come to Kansas to be ruinated and undone by grasshoppers."

Homesteaders who refused to quit—and they were in the majority—were faced with a hard winter. Many had no money, no credit, no food; some had no fuel or clothing. For the first time in the nation's history, the federal government offered relief to farmers, the Secretary of War issuing a "grasshopper appropriation" for the purchase of food and clothing to be "divided among the naked."

Funds were quickly exhausted, and appeals were made to more fortunate citizens in other states to help with offers of food and clothing. Several western states issued Grasshopper Bonds to relieve their desperate people. Nebraska passed a Grasshopper Act naming the insect as Public Enemy Number One, requiring every able-bodied male between the ages of sixteen and twenty to serve as legalized vigilantes in a continuous war against the foe.

Western settlers fought the grasshopper hard in 1875. Minnesota established a bounty of fifty cents a bushel on the destructive insects. Happy farmers fastened boxes on their reaper platforms and drove around their fields until the boxes were full. One farmer who had an abundance of the insects chased his neighbors with a pitchfork when he discovered them "poaching grasshoppers" on his land. It was fun while it lasted. But the bounty was in the form of state scrip, and so many grasshoppers were turned in for collection that Minnesota went bankrupt.

Several inventions appeared simultaneously, one being a hopperdozer which was supposed to put the insects quietly to sleep. Some settlers banded together in military fashion and fought the invaders with brush brooms. According to a newspaper account, one such army was headed by a brass band: "As the people drove clouds of these pests before them, the band discoursed sweet music, and made the war a very interesting and amusing one. The army of citizens fought them all day long and returned at night in good order."

Finally the grasshoppers began to decline, and as is the frontier custom after a major crisis, an anonymous bard composed a grasshopper ballad—three hundred and fifty-five verses sung to the tune of "Buffalo Gals," with a turkey gobbler as folk hero.

And so, in spite of grasshoppers and the violence of Nature, western homesteaders endured and eventually came to prosperity. They experimented with new crops, eagerly sought improved varieties of wheat and corn, replaced their long-legged sway-backed scrub cattle with blockier, meatier animals. As a means of spreading information among themselves, they organized annual State Fairs. Because western states were large and transportation was poor, the early fairs were held in different towns in succeeding years.

At a Colorado fair held in Denver in 1876, farmers exhibited "all varieties of produce among which are mammoth squashes, beets, potatoes, and melons, besides some freshly cut grass measuring over six feet in height." Premiums included ten dollars for the "best-dressed buffalo robe dressed in Colorado by a white man."

Fair managers favored horse racing but frowned on such things as balloon ascensions and trapeze performers. "They should be left to the domain of the circus," said John Shaffer of Iowa in 1880. "They are no part and parcel of the purpose for which State Fairs were organized. People will come to a fair without them." But Mr. Shaffer admitted that farm families needed some amusement and recommended that side shows be permitted. "They will follow after a fair, anyhow, as persistent eagles will gather together about a carcass. If admitted inside the grounds, any indecent or unmoral exhibition can at once be driven away, or any vices practiced under the canvass can be apprehended and abolished."

As settlement continued, the more populous counties began holding county fairs, offering long and varied lists of awards. In addition to the usual livestock and crop prizes, awards were made for such entries as: best lady driver of single horse and double team, best display of evergreens, best ten pounds of Indian corn starch, best fancy painting in oil, best agricultural wreath, best map of the solar system.

Manufacturers of farm machinery and household goods were encouraged to display their wares, and were given medals for the best revolving horse hay rakes, corn shellers, horse collars and shoes, kerosene lamps, washboards, bar soaps, and artificial teeth—all of which reflected the deep-felt needs of hard-working farm families in the West.

By 1884, just ten years after the disastrous grasshopper year, the settlers of the western plains had proved the Great American Desert to be a myth. In that year they prospered while eastern farmers suffered alternate drouths and floods. In April, Henry Worrall, the Kansas caricaturist, had the pleasure of drawing a sketch of a gaily draped train loaded with grain—the gift of western farmers to flood sufferers back east. "The cars were rudely but effectively decorated with designs in color," reported *Harper's*

Weekly which published Worrall's drawing with an account of the event. The grasshopper—rampant and couchant—was much in evidence among the blazing banners.

Transportation, however, remained as a formidable obstacle to farm prosperity in the West. The Missouri was the only navigable river which flowed to markets in the east. And although five great railroads were spanning the continent, there were few branch or intersecting lines to serve thousands of square miles of farm land long distances from the rails. Thirty miles was a long day's journey. One hundred miles required at least a week to come and go by horse team—even longer by ox team.

A southwestern cattleman could drive his stock overland to trail town railheads, but a wheat farmer had to load his crop in wagons, and then after consulting his almanac, drive off across the prairie behind a 20-mule team headed for the nearest railroad stop or steamboat landing. If the almanac was in error and heavy rains caught his tandem wagons en route, the wheels soon bogged to the axles. And even if the weather held good, very likely there was no shelter or grain elevator at the railroad loading point.

Some western homesteaders acquired steam-powered farm machines before they were able to enjoy the benefits of steam-powered rail transportation. In December 1870 a settler near Hell Gate, Montana, wrote to the Wood, Taber & Morse Company, explaining that since railroads had not yet reached his region, "your engine is a rare sight in these mountains. Some of the old mountaineers have come down the valley and camped for two or three days to see the machine and listen to the whistle of my agricultural steam engine."

Before the end of the century, steam-powered machines were a common sight on prosperous prairie and mountain valley farms. Each year they seemed to grow more gigantic, moving like clanking prehistoric monsters across the big rolling land.

Successful wheat farming with the new and expensive machines required extensive acreage, and upon the vast land grants paralleling the railroads, bonanza farms began developing in the late 1870's. The Northern Pacific Railroad, which crossed the Dakotas, took the lead in this type of farming, operating farms as large as 100,000 acres in the valleys of the James and Red rivers.

"You are in a sea of wheat," one visitor wrote, "the railroad train rolls through an ocean of grain." Hundreds of horses, dozens of mammoth steam-powered machines, seeders, harvesters and threshers were required to operate these bonanza farms. "Even the telephone is brought into requisition for the management of such an estate."

Men as well as machines were needed to plant and harvest these endless acres of wheat. Records of one farm of 60,000 acres show that 150 men were hired for April plowing and 400 during August and September for harvesting. But only a few hands were necessary during the other nine months.

To meet this demand for seasonal labor, migratory harvesting crews moved north across the plains each summer—working the wheatfields from Texas to the Canadian border. Ironically, quite a few of these workers were unemployed cowboys, refugees from *bonanza* cattle ranches which collapsed after the blizzard of 1886.

"They reached our neighborhood in July," wrote Hamlin Garland who lived as a youth in the wheat country, "arriving like a flight of alien unclean birds, and vanished into the north as mysteriously as they had appeared. Some carried valises, others had nothing but small bundles containing a clean shirt and a few socks."

Flying dust, cracking whips, glistening straw, a ceaseless ringing humming—that was horse-power threshing as described by Garland. "The wheat came pulsing out the spout in such a stream that the carriers were forced to trot on their path to and from the granary in order to keep the grain from piling up around the measurer. There was a kind of splendid rivalry in this backbreaking toil—for each sack weighed ninety pounds."

Along with bonanza wheat farming, sheep ranching also prospered in the late 19th century. "The expenses are not heavy," said Major William Shepherd who made a study of the industry in 1885. "Two men can through the year easily drive two or three thousand sheep. The returns from wool and increase are not exaggerated at twenty-five per cent."

Many additional men were needed at shearing time, however, and sheep shearers like harvest hands followed the season north, shearing wool with hand clippers. Beginning in March they moved up from the southwest into the Rocky Mountain ranges, reaching the Canadian border by July. A good shearer could clip a hundred sheep a day, might earn ten dollars—very good pay in those days.

Sheepmen trailed their stock to grazing lands and to markets, but unlike cattlemen they did not swim the animals across rivers. A sheep-bridge was necessary for a river crossing. "It often consists of a single large pine tree, which has been felled, and directed in its fall across the stream. A rough balustrade is added, and a few stones are piled to make a ramp by which the sheep can mount readily on to the log. The banks of the river on either side, above and below the bridge, may be fenced, to prevent the sheep from pushing each other into the water when crowding to cross." Wethers or goats were trained to lead the crossings.

Not all the western cowboys had turned to harvesting, and certainly very few would drive or shear sheep. The cattle trade still flourished after a fashion, but the range was closed, and no more trail drives could be made across the fenced and furrowed land. Said old-time cowboy Teddy Blue: "Fences and sheep and settlers were coming in, and the old-time big cow outfits was going out, and nothing was like it used to be in anymore." The cowboys spent their time riding within fenced ranges, searching for stray calves to brand, or routing outlaw steers out of hiding places in brakes and arroyos.

Western stockmen also liked to experiment with new breeds of animals. Along the grassy coastlands of Texas, A. P. Borden imported the first Brahmins from India; out in the Panhandle and on the plains of Kansas other men crossbred cattle and buffalo. In Bastrop County, Texas, Bethel Coopwood and John Wesley Lanfeer started a camel breeding experiment, hoping to market their product to the army for transport use across the high dry trails of the southwest.

By the turn of the century, the trusty ox had practically disappeared. But the horse was in his glory. As the west filled with new settlers, demand for horses reached a peak.

The natural supply of wild mustangs was soon exhausted, and horse ranches developed into profitable enterprises.

But the big money crop from southwestern land during the last years of the frontier was cotton. Texas and Oklahoma took over cotton raising from the Old South, fields of green and white covering the former grazing lands of the Longhorns.

"Cotton is the surees crop to rais in Texas," a shrewd settler wrote to a friend back in Ohio as early as 1833. By the end of the century, the railroad yards at Houston each ginning season were clogged with long lines of box cars and flat cars stacked high with bales of cotton.

Underneath the rich cotton lands of the southwest were even greater treasures. The Indians had known of places where brown fluids seeped from the earth, oils which healed battle wounds and skin diseases. Around such seeps were invisible substances in the air that would burn forever—better than pine torches to light the night during times of tribal ceremonies. The first pioneers learned to use the brown fluids for softening leather, lubricating wagon axles, and making ointments. Most Texans despised the stuff; it ruined their water for drinking. In 1886, a rancher near San Antonio drilled 235 feet for water, hit oil instead. He was disgusted until he discovered he could use it for fuel around the ranch.

Then in 1894, a well being bored for water at Corsicana suddenly began spouting oil in a steady stream. It caught fire and started the first oil boom in the west. Corsicana was soon producing petroleum commercially—1,450 barrels the first year. Four years later production rose to more than half a million barrels.

The Corsicana boom encouraged other petroleum drilling in Texas, and on January 10, 1901, an oil gusher big enough to surprise even a Texan blew in just outside Beaumont. Spindletop, the gusher was called—the most famed well in the history of western petroleum.

The first showing of oil came at around the 800-foot mark, and Al Hamill, the driller, figured he might bring in a fifty-barrel well. With his old-fashioned rig, he drove down another two hundred feet. Suddenly the drill pipe shot up out of the casing and knocked off the crown block. "In a very short time," Hamill said afterwards, "oil was going up through the top of the derrick and rocks were shot hundreds of feet into the air. Within a very few minutes, the oil was holding a steady flow at more than twice the height of the derrick." Spindletop spilled oil all over the Texas landscape, a hundred thousand barrels a day.

In a few weeks Beaumont was running a high fever. Wooden oil derricks shot up like weeds. Population jumped from ten to thirty thousand. Tents, shacks, saloons and gambling houses sprang up as they had in the old cattle trail towns of an earlier generation. Land values soared from $40 to $1,000,000 an acre.

The railroads ran special week-end trains for tourists, and the obliging oil men arranged for new wells to be spouting over the derrick tops every Sunday to entertain the visitors.

But before long another field, Sour Lake, had surpassed Beaumont as a rough, tough boomtown in the true western tradition. This pool was so rich that derricks were built with their supports adjoining. "For surging energy," recalls Charlie Jeffries who worked there as a roustabout, "for unrestrained openness and diabolical conditions otherwise, Sour Lake was head and shoulders above anything Texas had seen up until that time or perhaps has seen since. A short while after operations began, a large part of the field was worked up into such a mess of mud as can hardly be imagined. In saloons, Sour Lake ranked high. These were of all sizes and quality; they had appropriate names. There was the House of Lords, a place where the big boys gathered and played pool and rowdied around. There was the Derrick Saloon, and there was the Big Thicket Saloon, and there was Dad's Saloon; this last was a noted hangout for black-legs and cutthroats. After payday, when a gang of pipe-liners came to town, especially if it happened to be a chilly, drizzly evening, the sidewalk for a block or more would be filled with jabbering, reeling men."

The West's oil fever soon moved into Oklahoma, where homesteaders of recent land rushes were having no easy time of it on 160-acre claims unsuited for plow-farming and too small to support range livestock. Many were selling the land off for a few dollars an acre.

Then in 1905 near a sleepy village which the natives called Tulsey Town, wild-catters made a big strike in the Glenn Pool. Gamblers and speculators and the new fraternity of oil men in their big hats and laced boots swarmed into the little town on the Arkansas River. Millions of barrels of oil poured out, breaking prices on the market for a time. The Glenn Pool changed Tulsey Town into Tulsa, Oil Capital of the World.

A mad search for oil spread north and west across the Great Plains, new strike following new strike. Any shift upward in oil prices set off new drillings, sometimes so frenzied that thousands of barrels flowed back into the earth for lack of storage tanks. Often the spouting wells caught fire and burned for days in ominous clouds of greasy boiling smoke.

California had small petroleum fields long before Corsicana and Spindletop were discovered in Texas. But boomtowns and oil fever were lacking; perhaps California was immune to oil fever after its wild goldrush days. Not until the Lake View gusher blew in and poured out 90,000 barrels a day did Californians go a little mad over oil. For months Lake View spouted completely out of control, the richest oil well of all time, the spray covering an area fifteen miles around. "We cut an artery down there," said the driller, "Dry Hole Charlie" Wood. "What we feared most was an early rain. A flash flood could have spread our ocean of oil down over the valley below. So we went up into the hills with an army of 600 men and damned up the mouths of canyons with earth walls twenty feet high and fifty feet thick. Down below we built storage for ten million barrels of oil." Nine million barrels ran into the Lake View reservoir before it could be controlled, a flood of oil that dropped the market price from fifty to thirty cents per barrel.

Half a century before the contagious oil fever struck in the West, pioneers had been searching for riches under the big rolling land. The original wildcatters were gold prospectors, miners with pans and cradles. Men without women, they traveled on foot alongside their trusty burros instead of behind yoked oxen in covered wagons. They traveled light with only a pick and shovel, and needed no rotary rig to wheedle fortunes from the tantalizing earth.

"Stalwart, muscular, dauntless young braves," Mark Twain described them. "Brimful of push and energy. But they were rough in those times! They fairly reveled in gold, whiskey, fights and fandangoes."

While homesteaders were plowing the land and prospectors were digging beneath its surface, another breed of men was at work in the forests. During the era of settlement following the Civil War, the logging industry was first centered in the Lake States of Michigan, Wisconsin, and Minnesota. Here in the vast white pine forests was born Paul Bunyan, legendary figure of western loggers. Here again, the ox is the forgotten pioneer, as in the case of the first homesteaders. Ox wagons brought in veteran loggers from the east, ox teams hauled food and supplies to set up the first lumber camps, and then they went to work skidding logs on go-devils over ice and snow to river landings. Paul Bunyan's best friend was Babe, the Blue Ox.

Like all outdoorsmen, loggers enjoyed eating, but one of their peculiar traditions was silence at mealtimes. Stewart Holbrook, historian of the lumber industry, says the origin of this custom of no talking at mealtimes is lost in history: "Some lay it to the cook's desire to have the men fill their gut and get out as quickly as possible." Any violation of the rule was quickly quelled by the cook, who tolerated no sound except the "champing of jaws."

"We seldom ever worked on Christmast," wrote Otis Terpenning, a Minnesota lumberjack. "Some spent their time in playing cards, And listing for the cheerie sound of the dinner horn, Saying come and eat, eat. The cook would always have something extry, and plenty of it. Their was roast beef brown gravy, Good home made bread, Potatoes, Shiny tins heaped with golden rings called fried cakes And close to them a punkin pie baked in a ten-inch tin about one and a half inch deep."

While their contemporaries, the cowboys of the southwest, were putting brands on cattle, western loggers were similarly designating ownership with log marks. Both barkmarks and end-marks were used, applied with branding axes. When logs came down tributary streams to the big river booms, sorters worked over the jamming mass of timber, sorting the various brands, which were then joined into rafts for further movement down to the mills. A log in a boom without a brand was like a maverick cow in a roundup; it was anybody's log. And lumber "rustlers" tempted by thousands of unguarded logs sometimes stole choice specimens, obliterating or changing the original brands, and then sold them to the highest bidders.

By the end of the 19th century—the end of western settlement—the logging industry had leaped from the Lake States to the Pacific slopes, from white pines to Douglas fir and Ponderosa pine and redwood. And through all these swiftly changing years, the lumberjacks kept the big rivers of the western land filled with the felled giants of its virgin forests—logs from which came the millions of feet of lumber that built the towns and cities beyond the Mississippi.

"A MAN CAN LOOK FARTHER AND SEE LESS . . ."

Conquest of the western plains began in earnest after the Civil War, under the benefits of the Homestead Act of 1862. Encouraged by flamboyant advertising, thousands of emigrants moved out upon the great empty land, into an awesome, surreal world of earth and sky. Here lay the land, waiting for the settler's plough. For some the prospect was a world of beauty and freedom, for others it was frightening, sometimes maddening in its loneliness and strangeness.

UNREMEMBERED PIONEER

Patient, plodding, stolid—never romantic. That was the ox. Western poets have sung no songs for this cud-chewing animal, now virtually extinct. But without their yoked oxen, thousands of homesteading families could never have plowed their first fields or hauled wood and water. And in the dark days of the settlers' first blizzardy winters, more often than not it was the dependable ox that was sacrificed for food to keep them alive until spring.

FIRST ARRIVALS *(on facing page, top)*

The young farming men with their women and children came from everywhere, bringing everything they owned—a few horses or oxen, a coop of poultry, seeds for planting, a plough.

"IT WAS A HARD TIME ON WEMAN . . ." *(on facing page, bottom)*

The new settlers used different words to explain why they moved west, but beyond all their words was the old American vision of a better life beyond the far horizon. "We wanted to come to a new country," said Susan Frances Lomax, "so our children could grow up with the country. . . . It was a hard time on weman; they staid at home and did the work while the men were on their ponies hunting or looking after stock."

WELL DIGGERS: "IT'S JUST AS NEAR TO WATER ONE WAY OR THE OTHER . . ."

Everything but land and sky was scarce on the early western homesteads. Water was usually the scarcest necessity of all. As soon as the settler marked his claim, he started searching for water. The nearest stream might be ten miles away, and water had to be hauled in barrels until a well could be dug. When asked why he persisted in hauling water nine miles instead of digging a well, one farmer replied: "It's just as near to water one way or the other, and I prefer to get mine along horizontal rather than perpendicular lines." Itinerant well drillers finally solved the water problem for most western settlers.

GATHERING BUFFALO CHIPS

Finding fuel for cooking and heating was another new problem for the plains settlers. During the first decade of settlement following the Civil War, buffalo chips were the surest and most common source of fuel. Gathered into wagons, carts, or wheelbarrows, the chips were stacked in ricks or piled under a shed to insure dryness. They would not burn when wet.

WINDMILLS WERE BIG

(on facing page, bottom)
Water was sucked out of the deep wells with windmills, and the first homesteaders built huge ones, assuming that the bigger the wheels the more water would flow. In some areas Dutch-type windmills were built (such as this one photographed in Kansas in the 1860's) and were used for milling grain as well as for pumping water.

HAY BURNER

When nothing else could be found, hay was used as fuel. Several ingenious hay-burner stoves were developed during the 1880's, but according to a common saying of the times, it required "two men and a boy to keep a hay fire going."

51

FOOT CORN PLANTER.

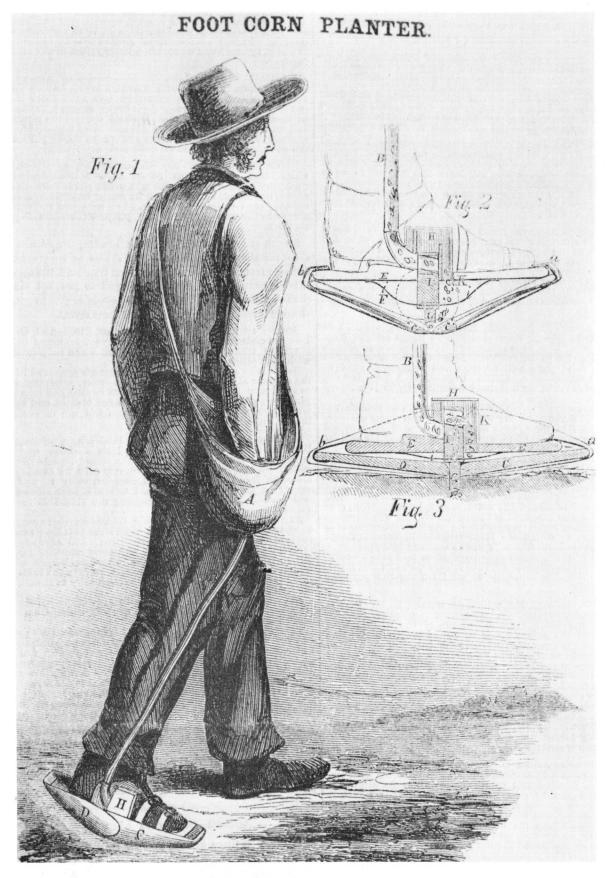

Fig. 1

Fig. 2

Fig. 3

THE MACHINE AGE: FOOT CORN PLANTER

The size of western farms encouraged mechanization. Because corn was grown on almost every farm, one of the first "machines" acquired was either a foot or hand corn planter. Instructions for operating the foot planter (*above*) were as follows: "This small, neat corn-planter is buckled on the foot. The operator carries the corn for planting in a small bag. The planter is connected to this bag by an elastic tube through which the seed corn is conveyed. When the foot is raised to make a step, a grain of corn drops into a chamber in the planter. When the foot comes down on the ground, the corn is pressed into the earth."

OX-DRAWN SELF-BINDER

As the settlers prospered, they began buying newly invented heavy machines. Across the expanding wheat country during the 1870's, reapers and binders and harvesters appeared in a variety of types and models. *Above* is the popular Marsh self-binder, drawn by oxen.

PRAIRIE FIRE

The "ocean of glory" that was the western prairie had its dangers to match its advantages. The highly publicized "savage Indians" were less fearsome than the violence of Nature. A common enemy was the prairie fire, a particularly awesome spectacle after nightfall. Prairie grass grew as high as a man's head, and during the rainless autumns it dried and browned under the sun until it was more inflammable than pitchpine. Once a fire was started, the only methods of defense were to set backfire, beat out the flames with brush, or run a drag over the line of fire.

WIND AND DUST

Twentieth century westerners may believe they have bigger wind and dust storms than the pioneer settlers, but early accounts of the plains country belie these modern claims. Newspapers were reporting dust storms as early as 1860: "The air was filled with bricks, barrels, boxes, tubs, signs, and boards which were blown about like chaff, and the dust so beclouded the air as to shut out the light of day."

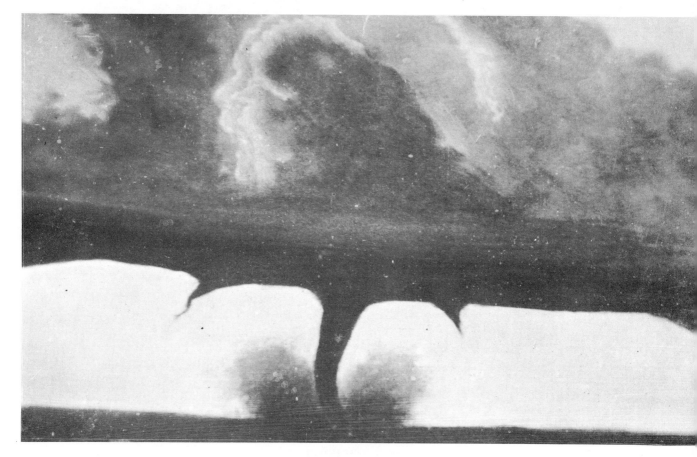

TWISTER

With its fearful roar and death-dealing funnel, the tornado was a terror to lonely plains dwellers. Photograph *above*, taken near Minot City, South Dakota, August 28, 1884, is believed to be the first ever made of a tornado.

BLIZZARD

Blizzard tales of the west are legion, and many of them are tragic. Inexperienced homesteaders were often caught away from home by blizzards, unaware until too late of how rapidly the temperature could drop and of how low was the visibility in a howling snowstorm on the plains. Train travelers, such as these on the Laramie Plains, were not much better off than a man on foot or horseback.

"DROUTHY KANSAS"

Stories of Nature's violence in the west drifted back to the east, reviving old tales of the Great American Desert. To counteract these stories, Henry Worrall of Topeka drew a charcoal sketch, "Drouthy Kansas," depicting huge corn stalks, grapes, watermelons, and potatoes. Worrall's caricature was reprinted all over the country, and tall tales about Kansas soon became a national fad.

WESTERN CORN

As photography came into common use, this new medium also helped spread the wonders of western agriculture.

YEAR OF THE GRASSHOPPER

In the summer of 1874 (long before flying saucers were invented) farmers all over the West began seeing strange silvery spots circling in the sunny skies. The silvery circles were millions of grasshoppers in flight, and before that summer ended, 1874 was known as the Great Grasshopper Year. The insects descended upon the land in columns 150 miles wide and 100 miles long. Efforts to save crops were futile. Hundred-acre cornfields vanished in a few hours. *Above* is farmer Swain Finch of Nebraska doing battle with the invaders.

MAJOR VICTORY FOR THE GRASSHOPPER

When a dark cloud of grasshoppers landed upon the Union Pacific tracks near Kearney, Nebraska, they stopped all trains, grease from the crushed insects setting locomotive wheels to spinning.

"SAVAGE INDIAN" AND HIS NEW ALLY

Homesteaders who refused to quit—and they were in the majority—were faced with a hard winter. Many had no money, no credit, no food; some had no fuel or clothing. For the first time in the nation's history, the federal government offered relief to farmers, the Secretary of War issuing a "grasshopper appropriation" for the purchase of food and clothing to be "divided among the naked." Cartoon above is an eastern periodical's view of the situation. As a matter of fact, the Indian was a minor irritant compared to his fearsome steed.

STATE FAIR, MINNESOTA

But in spite of grasshoppers and the violence of Nature, western homesteaders endured and eventually came to prosperity. They experimented with new crops, replaced their long-legged sway-backed cattle with blockier, meatier animals. As a means of spreading information among themselves, they organized annual state fairs. Manufacturers of farm machinery and household goods were encouraged to display their wares, and were awarded medals for the best revolving horse hay rakes, corn shellers, horse collars, kerosene lamps, washboards, and artificial teeth— all of which reflected the deep-felt needs of hard-working farm families in the West. *Above* is view of Minnesota's first fair held on Fort Snelling parade grounds at Minneapolis, 1860.

BONE HARVEST *(on facing page, bottom)*

Some settlers earned enough money to live through the winter by gathering the bones of buffaloes and other animals from the stripped land. The bones were symbolic but were not a direct result of the grasshoppers' ravages; they were converted into cash by shipping them east to fertilizer plants.

CORN TRAIN FROM WICHITA

By 1884, just ten years after the disastrous grasshopper year, the settlers of the western plains had proved the Great American Desert to be a myth. In that year they prospered while eastern farmers suffered alternate floods and drouths. In April, Henry Worrall, the Kansas caricaturist, had the pleasure of drawing a sketch of a gaily draped train loaded with grain—the gift of western farmers to flood sufferers back east. "The cars were rudely but effectively decorated with designs in color," reported *Harpers Weekly*.

HAULING WHEAT TO MARKET

Transportation, however, remained as a formidable obstacle to farm prosperity in the West. Although five great railroads spanned the continent, there were few branch or intersecting lines to serve thousands of square miles of farm land long distances from the rails. A wheat farmer had to load his crop in wagons and drive off across the prairie behind a 20-mule team headed for the nearest railroad stop or steamboat landing.

WHEAT WAGONS IN FARGO

Typical of wheat buying centers was Fargo, Dakota Territory, as shown in this 1879 photograph.

STEAM-POWERED PLOW

By energy and perseverance the western homesteaders overcame nature, isolation, and transportation difficulties. But the vastness of the prairie required power machinery for full conquest. The steam plow shown above was photographed in Martinez, California, in 1868, when grain was the principal farm product of that state.

PUFFING MONSTERS OF THE PRAIRIES *(on facing page)*

Before the end of the century, steam-powered machines were a common sight on prosperous prairie and mountain valley farms. Each year they seemed to grow more gigantic, moving like clanking prehistoric monsters across the big rolling land.

FARM MACHINERY HALL, 1879

In the larger towns, dealers such as J. R. McLaughlin of Fargo, Dakota Territory, built Farm Machinery Halls, where the latest in plows, wagons, and power machines could be inspected by interested settlers.

McCORMICK'S TWINE BINDER

The center of attraction during Fargo's Fourth of July celebration in 1881 was a fancy chariot advertising McCormick's new twine binder.

BONANZA FARMING

Successful wheat farming with the new and costly machines required increasingly extensive acreage, and upon the vast land grants paralleling the railroads, bonanza farms developed in the late 1870's. Threshing crew *above* is at work on the Dalrymple Farm in Red River Valley, a bonanza enterprise covering 100,000 acres.

THE PRESIDENT VISITS A BONANZA FARM, 1878

When President Rutherford B. Hayes toured the west in 1878, he stopped his special train to have a look at the famed Dalrymple Farm. "It was a sea of wheat, the railroad train rolling through an ocean of grain."

NOMADIC HARVESTERS

Men as well as power machines were needed to plant and harvest these endless acres of wheat. Records of one farm of 60,000 acres show that 150 men were hired for April plowing and 400 during August and September for harvesting. But only a few hands were necessary during the other nine months. To meet this demand for seasonal labor, migratory harvesting crews moved north across the plains each summer—working the wheat fields from Texas to the Canadian border. In photo *above,* man seated on left, second row, has a needle used for sewing wheat sacks thrust into his hat-band.

THRESHING WHEAT (on facing page, top)

Flying dust, cracking whips, glistening straw, a ceaseless ringing humming—that was power threshing as described by Hamlin Garland, who spent his early life in the wheat country. "The wheat came pulsing out the spout in such a stream that the carriers were forced to trot on their path to and from the granary in order to keep the grain from piling up around the measurer. There was a kind of splendid rivalry in this backbreaking toil—for each sack weighed ninety pounds."

HARVESTERS' CHUCKWAGON (on facing page, bottom)

Food in large quantities was the main requirement of the nomadic harvesters. Although a modified cow-country chuckwagon was developed for use on the big wheat farms, harvesters preferred their "vittles" cooked by females.

YOUNG BUNYANS AT WORK

As the loggers moved westward with settlement, they took their oxen with them to bring giant pines out of the mountain forests.

REPLACEMENT FOR BABE THE BLUE OX

But in a few years, funnel-stacked engines were puffing into formerly inaccessible areas on narrow-gauge rails. *Above* is a logging locomotive equipped with a fireproofer to control sparks.

A group of unusual log marks.

1. L. L. Hotchkiss, Ogemaw, 1881. 2. "Snowshoe"—Michigan Shingle Co., Roscommon, 1887. 3. "Q Tail Pig"—J. S. Quimby, Kent, 1869. 4. "Duck Murphy"—Murphy & Dorr, Saginaw, 1892. 5. "A One Boot"—C. N. Storrs Lumber Co., Muskegon Region, 1882. 6. "Slipper"—Peter Folmer, Kent, 1871. 7. Blodgett & Byrne, Muskegon, 1871. 8. "Baldy"—Johnston & Collins, Alpena, 1891. 9. "Bowl & Pitcher"—Muskegon Shingle & Lumber Co., Newaygo, 1883. 10. "Horse Head"—Richard Miller, Missaukee, 1900. 11. D. A. Ballou, Bay County. 12. "Snow Women"—Farr, Dutcher & Co., Muskegon Region, 1874. 13. "Ox Yoke"—S. H. Boyce, Muskegon Region, 1871. 14. James Wilson, Alpena, 1884. 15. "Pair of Legs"—Roskoff & Atherton, Muskegon. 16. William Webber, Muskegon, 1873. 17. "Canoe-man"—Street, Chatfield & Keep, Newaygo, 1882. 18. Shaw & Williams, Bay County. 19. "Elephant"—Muskegon Booming Co., Osceola, 1886. 20. "Fork for a Barn"—Farr, Dutcher & Co., Muskegon Region, 1874.

SORTERS

When logs came down tributary streams to the big river booms, sorters separated the various brands which were then joined into rafts for further movement down to the lumber mills.

LOG MARKS

While their contemporaries, the cowboys of the southwest, were putting brands on cattle, western loggers were similarly designating ownership with log marks. Both bark-marks and end-marks were used, applied with branding axes.

ROLLING DOWN THE RIVER

By the end of the 19th century—and the end of western settlement—the logging industry had leaped from the Lake States to the Pacific slopes, from white pines to Douglas fir and Ponderosa pine and redwood. And through all these swiftly changing years, the lumberjacks kept the big rivers of the western land filled with the giants of its virgin forests—logs from which came the millions of feet of lumber that built the towns and cities beyond the Mississippi.

CHAPTER THREE

THE STORY
OF A WESTERN TOWN

UNDER THE CANVAS of his covered wagon, the western overlander stowed a little of everything he required to start life in a new, raw land. Clothing, furniture, household equipment, weapons, seeds, medicine, schoolbooks, and a reserve of food were all intended to make the frontiersman independent. Such independence was short-lived. Powder and lead, if nothing else, tied the settler to the east. Conversely, the income from ranch or mine was worth little except as traded for products and manufactured articles necessary for life or desirable for comfort.

The link between the producer of the West, and the supplier-consumer in the east was the town. Often little more than a trading post, the western town supplied the needs of the settler, and took in return the raw material of the new land. The firm of Ridenour and Baker, frontier Kansas traders, reported that "Farmers came in from fifty to one hundred miles to trade. Several farmers would get together and send one team, and purchase a wagon load amounting to several hundred dollars. The buffalo hunters and trappers would come in with wagon loads of buffalo hides and tallow, and buy supplies. We bought hides, fur, grains, and all the farmer's produce."

Around such primitive enterprises grew the settlements, the centers of population which, in time, became chartered towns with names, and all the accoutrements associated with town life. Here were the centers of trade, of communication, transportation, of banking, and of native industries.

The location of a western town was usually determined by some natural advantage. Traders did not just pick a good view and settle on it. As overland trails were established, towns developed along the routes at fords, springs, junctions, and other natural stopping points. Waterfalls, heads of navigation, and approaches to mountain passes were geographical advantages favorable to the establishment of centers of population.

Some towns developed by a process of gravitation toward the old fur trade establishments and army posts founded by an earlier generation.

Mining towns were assembled as rapidly as new strikes were made, and as quickly abandoned. In October, 1861, the junction of Blue Canyon and Freezeout Gulch in eastern Oregon was a shelf of barren land like many others in the Powder River country. By the fall of 1862 the shelf supported a tent and cabin town of two thousand miners, traders, saloon keepers, and floaters. Auburn was a bustling place which had already hanged two men, one legally. A year later, half the population had rushed to the Boise Basin mines of Idaho, and Auburn was on the decline. In a decade the town was a "ghost," and today only the shelf of land remains.

Seaport towns with natural harbors were more permanent. San Francisco, most striking example of a city which survived the vagaries of a gold rush and desolation by disasters, was recognized as a town site in 1770. It became notorious when gold was discovered.

Bushrod Wilson, sailor and adventurer, described the town of San Francisco on July 3, 1850. "This place is a hard hole. Gambling, drunkenness, and immorality to excess, and a person that has just broke out in life is in great danger of being ruined here. Everything that will effect the senses is resorted to for base ends. The most enchanting music, the various forms of gambling, and obscene pictures, the allurements of women of the town, and drinking."

Wilson had his fling at the mines, and then left the scenes of iniquity to better his fortunes at what he believed would be the greatest city in the Oregon Territory. "Marysville," he wrote in 1851, "is at the head of steamboat navigation. We expect a steamer up here every day. We have a saw and grist mill here, fourteen houses, five stores, one tavern, two blacksmith shops, one cooper, one carpenter, one planing mill factory, and twenty buildings going up, where last year there was only two houses, one old log, and one split board house."

Bushrod Wilson's expectations were not fulfilled. His chosen site was not the head of navigation, and what navigation there was soon declined before a greater force, the railroad. The town of Marysville was just another country settlement kept alive by rural trade.

Geographical probabilities were sometimes ignored in the founding of western towns. In May, 1854, a sheriff, two doctors, a merchant, Indian agent, speculator, and two land agents crossed the Missouri river to the west bank. Here they erected a claim house of logs, and divided the land into town lots. By agreement, donations of property were assigned to the Methodist church, Masonic Lodge, and Odd Fellows. These founding fathers, members of the Council Bluffs and Nebraska Ferry Company, were engaged in the western frontier specialty of creating a town for speculative purposes.

Two years later, a steamboat crowded with emigrants stopped at the "Omaha City" landing. The town's entire population welcomed the vessel: "Were immigrants coming into the Territory? If so, how many and of what character and condition. Are there probably lot buyers? Do they come with cash, or with hoes and plows, or cards?"

Clark Irwin, one of the steamboat passengers, strolled to the Apex Saloon for a glass of beer. He paid for his drink with an imitation bill of the kind wrapped around a patent medicine bottle. The bill was accepted. "Money and town stock," concluded Irwin, "or any other nicely printed and ornamented paper, were superabundant and equally current."

The founders of Omaha were fortunate in their selection of a town site, though only two of them ever enjoyed residence there. Other town speculations were less rewarding. According to one account, "Intense fever was stirred in the blood of men by the hope and belief that a company of them, or possibly only one or two could get together, take a tract of government land worth $1.25 an acre, and simply by platting it into lots make it worth at once from $1000 to $3000 per acre."

All western towns, regardless of origin, depended on transportation for their existence. Trading posts and their successors, general stores, had to renew supplies and export the raw materials of trade. Before the day of the railroad, transportation services were handled by steamboat and ox-freight lines. Steamboats operated on every navigable river in the west. The Missouri river was the great western supply route. Fort Benton, dominated by the firm of Pierre Chouteau and Company of fur trade glory, was at the head of Missouri river navigation, and below that point the waterway was dotted with port towns whose main business was trans-shipment of steamboat freight via ox team.

Overland freighting in the West meant Russell, Majors and Waddell, greatest of all the freight companies, operating out of Nebraska City. Twenty-six wagons and 312 oxen made up one of their supply trains. Thirty bullwhackers kept the train moving, and the company furnished each man with a "pocket Bible as protection against moral contamination, two Colts revolvers and a large hunting knife as protection against Indians."

The ox-freight gradually gave way to the westward-pushing railroad as the major link between western towns and eastern markets. Gabe Wade of Atchison, Kansas, had been an enterprising freighter on the Denver route. When one of Gabe's oxen died on the trail, a wild buffalo was lassoed, and broken to yoke. The buffalo waxed fat in its new career, but ended its days as part of a barbecue celebrating the coming of the railroad.

The communication center of a western town was the express office. The government postal service was unable to cope with the rapid expansion and settlement of the western territories. Private initiative took over the job. Dominated by Wells, Fargo, the express companies delivered parcel, package and mail to the remote towns and mining camps scattered over plains and mountains. A few large companies operated overland, but most of them were local lines whose service depended on connections with the major organizations.

Alonzo Delano described the welcome arrival of an express in a California mining camp. "Every pick and shovel is dropped, every pan is laid aside, every rocker is stopped with its half-washed dirt, every claim is deserted, and they crowd around the store with eager inquiries, 'Have you got a letter for me?' "

As western towns grew, and population increased in density and variety, the institution of the trading post and general store was displaced by specialized enterprises. Butcher shops, drug and cigar stores, hay-grain-and-feed stores, real estate offices, banks, and saloons filled the needs of the community and surrounding country. Combinations of enterprise were common. Usually the furniture dealer doubled as undertaker, the local carpenter built coffins, the newspaper editor often read law or sold real estate. The hay and grain business was part of a livery stable, and the hotel operated a restaurant on the premises. As one groceryman put it, "You can't make a living selling groceries alone. We sell that line at cost to bring in trade for our other goods."

Manufacturers flourished in western towns, and faded with the coming of cheap railroad transportation. Many communities had their own flour mills. Furniture manufacturing, and the allied skill of carriage and wagon building were profitable frontier enterprises. Some westerners manufactured farm equipment, others found breweries more economic. Boots and shoes were made in the West before it became cheaper to import them. Woolen mills were founded in favorable areas, and flourished on government contracts for blankets delivered to the reservation Indians. Iron works were incorporated, and abandoned. Meat packing plants, notably that of the Marquis de Mores of Medora, Dakota, were built in defiance of the great slaughtering centers of Kansas City and Chicago.

Few western industrial efforts survived eastern competition. Processing of fish, lumber, fruits and vegetables, or the building of wooden ships was always economic near the source of raw material, but in general the western settler delivered the products of his land to the middle West and East. The western towns learned not to depend on manufacturing as a way of life.

Western banks, too, reflected the dependence of the frontier on eastern institutions. Banks rose in confidence, and fell whenever the winds of financial panic blew from the East. Bank currency issued in the West was, in the words of one printer, "The substance of things hoped for, the evidence of things not seen." When a Missouri river steamboat captain tried to bargain for a few cords at a woodyard, the proprietor asked, "What kind of money do ye tote?"

"The best on earth—the new Platte Valley Bank."

"If that be so, I'll trade cord for cord."

The one town institution which most nearly reflected the temper of the West was the newspaper. "A press, ink, paper, type, pistols and coffee" represented the investment necessary for a paper in frontier days. Ability to write well, or previous experience was secondary. Under such favorable circumstances the editor and his press followed the covered wagon before the dust of the emigrants had settled.

Independent newspapers did not exist. It did not pay to be independent; an editor's income came from legal notices and job printing rather than from commercial advertising, and political backing assured prosperity. Personal journalism was the frontier style, and involved publication of scurrilous remarks about rival editors. "There is not a brothel in the land that would not have felt itself outraged by the presence of the *Oregonian* of the week before last," wrote Asahel Bush, editor of the *Statesman* from Salem, Oregon. "It was a complete tissue of gross profanity, falsehood, and meanness." One pioneer journalist was described as "formerly editor, proprietor, printer, compositor, roller boy, extra seller, libeller, item gatherer, affidavit maker, slanderer general, and pimp generalissimo."

Now and then editorial remarks concluded with personal violence. George W. Clark of the Van Buren, Arkansas, *Intelligencer* referred to his colleague, John S. Logan of the *Frontier Whig* as "Big Mush." Logan responded with "Toady Clark." The two inventive editors fought a duel with rifles at sixty paces. Two shots were fired by each, but no one was hurt. "The smell of powder and bad marksmanship are said to have led to a reconciliation."

The precarious, yet congenial atmosphere of frontier journalism was recalled by an 1857 Kansan. "A visit to the printing office afforded a rich treat. On entering the first room on the right hand, three law shingles were on the door; on the one side was a rich bed—French blankets, sheets, table cloths, shirts, cloaks and rugs, all together; on the wall hung hams, maps, venison and rich engravings, onions, portraits and boots; on the floor were a side of bacon carved to the bone, corn and potatoes, stationery and books; on a nice dresser case stood a wooden tray half full of dough, while crockery occupied the professional desk. In the room on the left—the sanctum—the housewife, cook, and editor lived in glorious unity—one person. He was seated on a stool, with a paper before him on a plank, writing a vigorous knockdown to an article in the Kickapoo *Pioneer,* a paper of a rival city. The cooking stove was at his left, and tin kettles all around; the corn cake was adoin', and instead of scratching his head for an idea, as editors often do, he turned the cake and went ahead."

Such were the towns and town institutions of the early West. Many flourishing centers vanished with a sudden exodus of population; others died slowly of economic attrition. Some tasted momentary glory only to subside into semi-oblivion. Those which survived outgrew the pioneer phase, battled flood and fire, and assumed their place in the western scheme of civilization.

DEPENDENT PIONEER

The western pioneer was independent only until the supplies in his covered wagon ran out. After that, the settler looked to the east to supply him with goods necessary for life, and desirable for comfort. In exchange, the pioneer offered the products of the new land. The major link between East and West was the town. McGrew and Smyth of Holton, Kansas, advertised in 1874 that they were the place to buy and sell.

TRADING POST

In the early West, a town was sometimes little more than a trading post. To the trader came fur trappers with their pelts, buffalo hunters with hides and tallow, farmers with grain, miners with dust. To all these the trading post was a place to get powder and shot, tobacco, coffee, clothing, beans, liquor and news. Smith and Hagy's store, Huntley, Montana Territory (*above*) was a trading post in the frontier style.

TOWNSITE

Location of western towns was often based on geographical factors. Fords, springs and junctions on the overland routes, natural stopping places, became townsites. Waterfalls were recognized as likely spots for settlement. Oregon City in 1858 *(above)* at the end of the Oregon Trail, and at the falls of the Willamette river seemed destined to be the major city of the region. No one could have predicted that Portland, a few miles downstream, would outgrow the city by the falls.

OPHIR HOLES, GOPHER HOLES, LOAFER HOLES

Mining towns were located by a process of natural selection, and abandoned as rapidly as founded. Western geography is punctuated with their names once known to thousands, and now forgotten. Described as "Ophir holes, gopher holes and loafer holes," mining communities were a mixture of success, frustration, and despair. Pioneer City *(above)*, first gold camp in Montana, lived longer than most, but its glory faded when the nuggets were gone.

ONE HUNDRED YARDS WIDE, A MILE LONG

Terrain meant nothing when a gold town was on the make. Houses, stores, streets were crowded into canyons and gulches, or suspended on steep hills. Burke, Idaho *(above)*, had a main street so narrow the awnings had to be raised to let the train go by.

A LIVELY CAMP

Some mining camps outlived their growing pains, and developed into commercial and political centers. Helena, Montana *(above)*, was on July 9, 1865, "a lively camp. Three thousand people were there. The saw and hammer were busy in putting up cabins and storehouses, and in constructing sluice boxes for the washing out of gold. Trade was lively, saloons crowded, hurdy gurdy dance houses in full blast. There was suspended on the limb of a tree a man hung by the Vigilante committee the night before, the eighth specimen of similar fruit encased in leather boots that tree had borne in so many months."

HARD HOLE

Seaport towns enjoyed special advantages. San Francisco was recognized as a likely townsite by 1770. It became notorious when gold was discovered, but the harbor was worth more than the mines of the interior. "A hard hole," said Bushrod Wilson of the above scene in 1850.

LIKELY SPOT ON THE RIVER BANK

Geographical probabilities were sometimes ignored in the establishment of western towns. In 1854 eight men crossed the Missouri river to the Nebraska side, erected a log claim cabin, and divided the empty land into town lots. Property was assigned to the Methodist church, Masonic Lodge, and Odd Fellows. The town *(above)* was named Omaha City in 1862 after the nearest tribe of Indians.

LITHOGRAPHED MENDACITY

The business of buying a piece of government land and increasing its value a thousand-fold by platting it into lots and calling it a town was popular among frontier speculators. John J. Ingalls, Massachusetts lawyer, was attracted in 1856 by a colorful lithograph of Sumner, Kansas Territory *(above)*. When Ingalls arrived, he found little but platted Kansas prairie. In later years as Senator from Kansas he recalled the attractive advertisement as a "chromatic triumph of lithographed mendacity."

HEAD OF NAVIGATION

All western towns depended on transportation for their continued existence. Before the coming of the railroad, transportation service was handled by steamboat and ox-team freight. The Missouri river was the supply line of the West. Fort Benton, at the head of the Missouri river navigation, was established in 1846 as supply post for the American Fur Company. During the Montana gold rush of the 'sixties, the site boomed, and a town grew up around the post. Steamboats loaded with freight and anxious miners disembarked here. The name Choteau, attached to the hotel, testified to the fur trade origins of the town.

SUPPLY DEPOT

Below Fort Benton, the waterway was dotted with port towns whose main business was to maintain the flow of supplies from the East. Steamboats were the lifeline of the frontier. The *Eclipse* is docked at the Third Street landing, Bismarck, Dakota, 1876.

LAND FREIGHT

From Bismarck and other Missouri river points freight was hauled overland by ox team to the interior settlements. Pierre, Dakota Territory, was the port of entry for the Black Hills mining region. Fred T. Evans ran bull trains from the river boats to the gold town of Crook City in 1877 *(above)*. Evans was a large, capable man with a vocabulary even an ox could understand.

96

MULE TRAIN

Towns too remote for wagon trains were supplied via mule-back. Mining towns in the mountains were likely to have to depend on the mule. Everything from bacon to billiard tables was packed across the narrow trails that connected remote settlements with the outside world. The art of packing, a special skill developed largely by the Mexicans, was euphonious with Spanish terms like cargadore, aparejo, suadera and cincha. Some of these terms were mangled into English. The pack train *above* has just arrived at a Colorado mining town.

FEMALE BULLWHACKER (on facing page, top)

On the same route with Evans was Mrs. Knutson, *left of center* in the picture, one of the few female bullwhackers in the West. Her husband worked a homestead claim, while she, "too weak to farm," carried her baby and drove freight into Rapid City. Greatest of the western freight companies was Russell, Majors and Waddell, who operated out of Nebraska City. The bull-whackers in this outfit were not ladies. The company supplied them with pocket Bibles "as protection against moral contamination."

FREIGHT STOP (on facing page, bottom)

Along the routes of the ox-team freighters, small settlements were established at natural stopping places—water supply and pasturage. The names and locations of many such temporary halts have long disappeared into history. Bakeoven (*illustrated*) in eastern Oregon, was named after the enterprising activities of a freighter who was stranded with a load of flour, his team driven off by Indians. He built an oven, baked bread with his flour, and sold the product to miners traveling along the road.

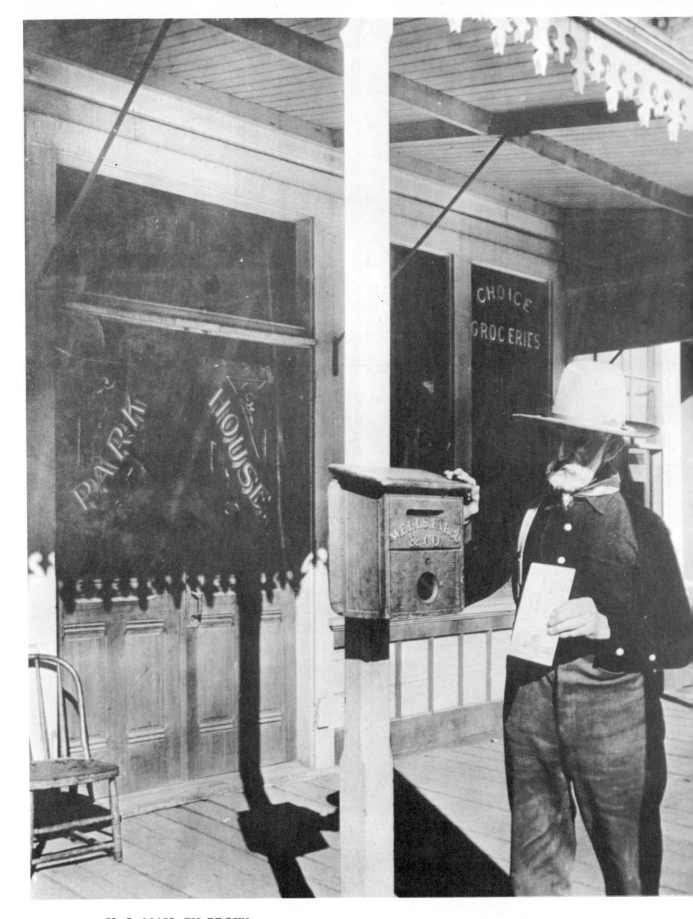

U. S. MAIL BY PROXY

Communication center of the western town was the express agent. The government post office was unequal to the task of providing mail and parcel service to the scattered settlements of the vast area beyond the Missouri. Express companies, founded by private enterprise, took over the work. Best known of the companies was Wells, Fargo, which operated overland, and by connections with local concerns penetrated wherever express service was established.

BEEKMAN EXPRESS

Both Wells, Fargo and local express companies were represented in the major western towns by agents who maintained offices in general stores, banks, or other establishments. The Beekman Express of Jacksonville, Oregon, operated in the 1850's from the Beekman bank *(above)*. To this office came miners with gold dust to be weighed and shipped; into this office came letters and packages addressed to the miners and settlers of southern Oregon and northern California.

THE CUSTER ROUTE

Serving the Black Hills population was the Northwestern Express, Stage and Transportation Company of Deadwood *(above)*. Via the "Custer Route" to Bismarck, a miner could transport mail, packages, freight, or himself anywhere in the world.

WAYSIDE HOTEL

For the accommodation of human traffic, most western towns boasted a hotel, or stage stop. Overcrowding was no problem; wayfarers usually carried a blanket or two and floor space was available for fifty cents. One such hostelry was known as the "Six Bit House," the charge being two bits each for supper, bed and breakfast. The Belle Fourche stage station *(above)*, stockaded against Indian attack, offered shelter to stage passengers from the Black Hills.

BED BUGS AND BROAD GAUGE RATS

Where transient traffic was heavy, more pretentious hotels flourished. The Capitol Hotel at Bismarck, Dakota, in 1876 *(above)*, was well located. The town enjoyed considerable steamboat and stage business and was hard by Fort Abraham Lincoln, outfitting point for many army expeditions. Well kept, such hotels were comfortable. Usually they suffered from invasions of "bed bugs and broad gauge rats."

BEANS AND BROOMS

As western towns grew, the familiar all-purpose trader's store disappeared, and specialty stores supplied the demand for eastern goods. Tinned and sacked foods were the major stock in trade of the early groceries. Fresh vegetables were sold in a limited season, if at all. In the tinned line a patron could get beans packed in Chicago, or oysters from Baltimore.

WALLPAPER AND CRAYONS

The western appetite for the comforts of life was satisfied by a shopping tour in town. E. A. Grant's store in Fargo, Dakota *(left)*, provided the pioneer of 1876 with wallpaper, stationery, crayons, stereoscopic views, beauty cream, and other refinements not usually associated with life on the plains.

GOOD VIRTUE GAINS BIG PROFIT

An institution peculiar to western towns was the Chinese store. Tea, canned fish, firecrackers, opium, and other esoteric specialties were offered for sale. Excluded from occidental society, the Chinese maintained much of their native culture in the foreign land. The wall mottoes flanking the door at the rear of the shop *(above)* assure the proprietor that Broad Spirit nourishes high ability to sell and buy on good terms, and that Good Virtue gains big profit and good prospects.

GENTS' FURNISHINGS

Even remote settlements were invaded by merchants looking for profitable business. J. L. Niebergall set up a men's clothing shop in Cripple Creek, Colorado *(above)*. The mining population was in no position to practice the art of making or remaking clothes. For their boots, shirts, coats and hats they went to Niebergall.

TOBACCO AND SASSAFRAS

Drug and cigar stores were, in frontier days, just that. They did not sell kitchen equipment, wagons, or sporting goods. They were notable for the modest size of their soda fountains, and variety of patent medicines. Their drugs and nickel cigars combined to give the stores an indefinable smell.

THE BUTCHER

Butcher shops in western towns offered patrons a choice of tame and wild meat. John Audubon visited western butcher shops to find specimens for his drawings. Customers looking for meat could choose between the usual beef and pork, or buy a bear steak, buffalo hump, antelope, venison, prairie chicken, or whatever the professional hunters had brought in.

THE BAKER

Frontier bakers found business especially good among bachelors. The miners of the Coeur d'Alene region were too busy to leave their diggings, and were well served by the mule-back bakery *(above)*. Fresh bread was a treat no miner could resist, even at a dollar a loaf.

THE CARRIAGE MAKER

There were no western industrial towns. A few industries were established to fill demands not easily satisfied by imports, but when cheap transportation brought the factories of the East into competition with the West, such manufacturing was no longer economic. Wagon and carriage works were founded at widely separated points, from Iowa *(above)* to California. Western wagon works produced durable goods, specially suited for local conditions.

WOOLEN MILL

The manufacture of woolen goods flourished for a time in the West. Blankets were a major product, most of them intended for the Indian trade. The government usually included blankets on its list of Indian annuity payments, and woolen mills in the West were given profitable contracts.

IRON WORKS

Bar iron, strap iron, nails and wire were much in demand on the frontier. The demand could either be filled by shipment from the East, or by utilization of iron deposits in the West. The Oregon Iron Works, Oswego *(above)*, tried to capture the Pacific coast market. Neither the iron deposits nor the available coal were of high enough quality to assure profitable operation.

MONEY AND CREDIT

Mark of progress in any western town was the bank *(above)*. Prairie banks issued their own currency, described by one printer as "the substance of things hoped for, the evidence of things not seen." Gold dust was more dependable as currency. Western banks were closely tied to land and cattle prices, unstable at best, and financial indigestion was a chronic condition among pioneer establishments.

A LIKENESS FOR THE HOME FOLKS

Unwitting chronicler of the West was the town photographer. In his home studio, or as a summer itinerant, the photographic artist was early on the western scene: The urge to send a likeness to the folks back in the "states" was strong among the pioneers, especially the bearded miners. The reaction of one fond father, Samuel G. Crawford of Havana, N. Y., was forthright. "We received Ronald's ambrotype, and had his name not been inside, we would not have known it. When he left home he was a smooth-faced, good-looking boy, and he sends home the likeness of an ourangoutang with the upper part of his face shaved!!" The E. H. Train studio of Helena, Montana *(above)*, did a brisk business among pioneer families.

SOLID CITIZEN

The variety that characterized western town life favored the pioneer who was adept at a number of skills or trades. John Bentley *(above* with family) was a carpenter, undertaker, sawmill owner, sheriff, and United States Marshall. "One time during a diphtheria epidemic," wrote Bentley, "I worked all night making five caskets for the children of Mr. and Mrs. Ben Ogle. The five of them died of this disease and were buried the same day. My wife held the light for me that night as I made those coffins, and it was morning before I finally completed them." John was familiarly known as "Two-toot Bentley," after the signal for his being wanted at the lumber mill.

DEADLINE

Establishment of a newspaper was a landmark in the progress of a western town. Little capital, a minimum of equipment, and a strong personality were the requirements for a country weekly. Even so, newspapers changed hands frequently for personal or political reasons. The first editor of the Prescott, Arizona *Miner* (office *right*), was killed by Apache Indians. His successor, John Marion, was more careful and produced a lively paper frequently quoted in California dailies.

INNER SANCTUM

The spirit of the West was most clearly reflected in the columns of frontier newspapers. On the pages of the weeklies are preserved the history of the land and the men who conquered it. Western editors were well suited to their picturesque environment. According to one description, the inside of a newspaper office "afforded a rich treat—hams, venison, rich engravings, onions, portraits and boots hung on the wall . . . in the sanctum the housewife, cook and editor lived in glorious unity—one person." Clark Wood of the Weston, Oregon *Leader (above)*, enjoyed a long and benign reign over the fortunes of the little country town. He was tempted by the big city, but returned to his stove and hand press, king of the locals and job work, the voice of a western town.

CHAPTER FOUR

THE FINER THINGS IN LIFE

ALVIRA RAYMOND, wife of an Indian mission employee in the Oregon country, wrote her sister in 1842, "One thing that is discouraging is that the natives of this land are dying off very fast, and all we do for them must be done shortly. A thing that encourages us is that this country is filling up with those who need the gospel more, if possible, than the heathen."

Few western emigrants were so fortunate as to have an organized mission waiting for them when they arrived at their new home. Overland wagon trains often included "preachers" as members of the company, and when the Sunday "lay bye" was observed, a service might be held. One such occasion, along the Snake river in 1862, was described by Evans S. McComas of Iowa, "Had preaching in our correl by Capt. Bristle, the fighting Capt. of the Iowa City train. Had a sermon from the 8 chapt. and 28 verse of Romans. It was a curious group for to be at church, the men with Bowie knives and revolvers to their belts, in their shirtsleeves and buckskin pants—with one exception. One old fellow sit up, stiff as a churn dash, with a starched shirt and linen coat on. It did not look much like a basket meeting in the States."

The frontier preachers were a miscellaneous lot, and their reasons for migrating westward were not always spiritual. The Rev. James Croke, S.J. noted in 1854 that many of the settlers "*Are* or *have been* preachers. These gentry, finding that farming *pays better* than preaching, have renounced the pulpit for the plough." Father Croke overlooked the circumstance that many of these "renegades" were self-ordained, and that certain Protestant denominations regarded missionary work as impertinent interference with the predestined will of God.

The major church bodies sent representatives to the frontier to preach, marry, baptize, bury, and comfort. The successful missionaries forgot their ecclesiastical feuds in a common effort to ameliorate the spiritual and social condition of the settlers. The first Episcopal communion service in Virginia City, Montana, welcomed Baptists, Methodists and Lutherans to the Lord's Table.

When no church building was available, services were held in private homes, in stores, saloons, and billiard parlors. The literal hat was passed by zealous deacons who sometimes obtained contributions at gun point. Settlements cooperated in the erection of religious "Pantheons" for the use of all denominations—"Mormons excepted." Divine worship was attended by emigrants of all and no creeds. "I enjoyed your preaching," said one honest lady, "but I do not believe a word you said about Christ being God; however, if you will come with me and my boys, we will give you a dinner, the best we have."

The itinerant preacher, or circuit rider, was a frontier institution carried west in the same pattern that had developed east of the Missouri. The camp meeting, revival, "protracted meeting," and related devices associated with certain denominations were westernized. According to Ed Howe, "The first wickedness I ever heard of came with attendance on these camp meeting, for on their edge collected strange men who sold keg beer, and whisky in bottles, and their patrons engaged in rough language and fighting."

It was not always wise to preach hell-fire to the westerners, or be too critical of their surface morals. One group of miners, anxious for the services of a permanent minister, assured Anglican Bishop Ethelbert Talbot, "We boys will treat him white—only don't send us no stick."

Western "sky pilots" sometimes sacrificed their lives in the cause of Christ. Valentine Rightmyer, Methodist minister of Gold Hill, Nevada, died April 11, 1863 of starvation, "having a small salary, a large family, and too much pride." Preacher Henry Weston Smith, first to carry the Gospel to Deadwood, posted a notice in his cabin door, August 20, 1876, "Gone to Crook City to preach, and God willing will be back at three o'clock." God was in this instance not willing. Preacher Smith was killed by Indians a few miles out of town.

Religious specialists, seers, spirit-talkers, and deviates found the West a fair field. They were usually regarded with curiosity or cautious amusement. The "Bulgarian Monk" of Bay Horse, Idaho, descended on that community from time to time. Dressed in his version of apostolic garb, the Monk pronounced jeremiads over the sinful miners, and returned to the mountains to gather fresh information for his next visit. The American Society of Infidels had a large membership in the West. Certain local infidels, according to one report from Iowa, "wore long hare and looked like Crist."

Education as well as salvation was important to the pioneer cultural effort. School books, advised an overland guide, were important to an emigrant family with children. The problem of educating the young in the new country was more complicated than a matter of book shortages. There was also a lack of teachers. In homes with educated parents, the children learned to read and write by the hearthside. In settled communities families cooperated to build a schoolhouse, hired a teacher, and hoped for the best. The best was not much. Teachers were often little better educated than their pupils. Well-educated persons on the frontier could find more profitable employment clerking in a store. Thomas J. Dimsdale of Rugby and Oxford was paid two dollars a week per child for teaching school in Virginia City, Montana, during the winter of 1863-1864. Dimsdale found better employment as editor of the Montana *Post*.

Early settlers were by no means united in the notion that universal education was a good thing. "Our teacher," wrote an observing pupil in 1863, "has just about taught as long as any man can in this town, and consequently is just about played out. The directors hired him at $40 per month. The people got into one of their contrary ways, and kept their children from school."

Writing schools, spelling schools, singing schools and painting schools were available on occasion when an itinerant teacher offered short-course specialties. Facility in the Spencerian hand, "training in the vocal voice," and quantities of rose-ornamented china-ware were the tangible results of such educational diversions.

"Higher" education on the frontier was dominated by the "academies." Some of these establishments never got beyond the realm of hope; others withered after the publication of a few catalogs and appeals for financial aid. The condition of common schools in the West did not provide enough material for institutions of higher learning. Not until late in the nineteenth century were the frontier states able to support worthwhile colleges, and a few universities. Even then, as one professor testified, "The raw material is very raw."

The informal lyceum, debating society, and later the Chautauqua provided cultural opportunities at varying levels. According to one Kansas emigrant, "I have listened to most animated and profound discussions of the immortality of the soul, whether the Bible was inspired, foreordination, transsubstantiation . . . the doctrines of John Calvin, and the infallibility of the pope." Hours of serious debate were held over whether true beauty was to be found in nature or in art, whether fire was more destructive than water, and whether the fear of punishment was a greater incentive than the hope of reward. Fundamentally, the "cultural" society served a social purpose, well expressed in a note received by a young Iowa maiden, "Will you go to Literary with me a-Friday night? If so, please let me know by a-Tuesday night."

The lack of general education in the West was reflected in the condition of the arts generally. What literature, music and drama existed was largely imported. There was almost no sustained creative activity. The overland diarist, quite unconsciously, was the first frontier literary figure. A few of the early travel journals were deliberately assembled for publication as guide books. Most of them were written for their keepsake value; their literary or historical merit was discovered by a later generation.

The frontier poet was a special case. The literary urge quiescent in the breast of the emigrant erupted early in poetry production. When newspapers were established, the settler-poets showered local editors with political, social, and religious opinions in verse. A few of the grass-roots poets attempted flights of fancy; others felt that humor was their forte. All of them imitated popular eastern poets.

Now and then territorial verse writers defied literary probabilities and produced either quantity or quality enough to deserve recognition. Of the quantity school was Captain Jack Crawford, dubbed the "Poet Scout." The Captain dashed off reams of verse on frontier themes, and made his living as a free-lance army scout. Jack published his work, and tried in vain to sell it. There were no remainder houses to resolve Jack's predicament, so he resorted to the inducement of "autograph, presentation" copies, with additional holograph poems on the flyleaf.

Captain George Waynefleet Patten, western Indian fighter, known to his fellow-soldiers as "He-he-be-God Patten, was unofficially considered "poet-laureate of the United States Army," in recognition of his western "poetical effusions." Patten was fond of "The Emigrant's Dying Child" and similar lugubrious themes. Sitting Bull, the great Sioux medicine man, was a poet, at least by repute. His "Works" in the original Latin, French and German, edited by a military friend, went through two editions, more than common for poets.

Joaquin Miller and Eugene Field were poets of the frontier environment, respected for their quality. Miller was not popular in his home territory of California and Oregon, but was feted as a literary prodigy in the east and abroad. He doubled as his own press agent, and his success in that line outran his literary talent.

Native frontier fiction writers left almost no impression on early western literary history. Most states and territories saw one or two outbursts of fiction, like that of Margaret Jewett Bailey's *Grains, or, Passages in the Life of Ruth Rover*. This true-confession novel, published in Oregon in 1854, caused a temporary sensation, but did not found a literary movement.

Edgar Wilson "Bill" Nye, hailed as a humorist, practiced his style in the young city of Laramie, Wyoming. Nye combined his breezy talents with the reputation of James Whitcomb Riley. Between them they published a railway guide. "What this country needs," said Nye, "is a railway guide which shall not be cursed with a plethora of facts or poisoned with information."

Though the pioneers wrote little, they read much. "My literature is a volume of Shakespear, Dr. Gunn's Family Physician, and an agricultural report," wrote a young lady in 1870. "I have read the Shakespear till I feel my morals are damaged, Dr. Gunn till I am a first-class family physician myself, and the agricultural report till I can discuss stock and soil with anyone."

Literary traffic in books and periodicals from the East was surprisingly heavy on the frontier. "Horace Greeley's Weekly Tribune furnished our political economy, and Harper's Weekly was a regular visitor," recalled one Kansan, "while Petroleum V. Nasby furnished the humor of the day." Booksellers' records and newspaper advertisements indicate that the settlers pined for and bought the same mixture of classic and yellow-back literature popular in the "states."

The westerner who wanted more than the good cheer of a book could attach him-self to the Freemasons, Odd Fellows, Red Men, or Good Templars, social importations from the East. The frontier produced some home-grown organizations, notably the E Clampus Vitas of the California miners, and the P.E.O., devised by two young ladies of Iowa Wesleyan college in 1869. Few pioneer biographies could be written without mention of membership in one or more fraternal associations.

Greater than the impact of prose, poetry, or social assembly was the cultural effect of frontier drama. Travelling players penetrated the mining towns, villages, and cross-roads settlements. Towns with no church or school boasted an "Opera House."

"An enormous nose and a powerful voice" was enough to please some western audiences. Others were more critical. In 1881 the divine Bernhardt played *Camille* in Tootle's Opera House, St. Joseph, Missouri. As Ed Howe of the Atchison *Globe* saw the performance, "At exactly 8:31 last night Sara Bernhardt made her appearance on the stage of Tootle's Opera House, walking down the centre as though she had but one joint in her body, and no knees . . . Her dress was of white and costly stuff, and cut so low in front that we expected every moment that she would step one of her legs through it . . . With reference to *Camille* in French, it is about as interesting to an American as five acts of a Chinese drama running three months."

Faced with the spectacle of Adah Isaacs Menken "in pink tights, lashed to a horse," playing in *Mazeppa* the audience of the Virginia City, Nevada, theater was moved to frenzy, and presented the lady with a two-thousand-dollar gold bar.

Much frontier theater was crude, "thirty lightning acts in succession, no long waits." The traveling companies starved from one engagement to the next, though as Chris Fletcher, theater manager of Hartville, Wyoming complained, "As soon as they get the wrinkles out of their bellies they go temperamental."

Theaters doubled as gambling houses and dance halls. The Bella Union, first theater in Deadwood, specialized in variety acts. When the show was over, the house was cleared for action of various kinds. The seventeen curtained boxes of the Bella Union were then used by the female players, as one chronicler phrases it, "to sell themselves."

Variety and vaudeville gradually centered in the larger western towns and cities. One-night stands by second-rate companies kept the hopes of many small town opera houses flickering, but around the turn of the century the Keystone Cops on the screen pushed *Uncle Tom's Cabin* from the stage.

The Bishop Is Coming!

LET US ALL TURN OUT AND

HEAR THE BISHOP

Services in George and Human's Hall tomorrow, Sunday, at 11 A.M. and 8 P.M.

PLEASE LEAVE YOUR GUNS
WITH THE USHER

Wallace, Idaho. Miner Print.

CHURCH IN THE WILD COUNTRY

Churches in the new West had to wait their turn. Houses and stores were built first as a matter of practical survival. Few communities had enough members of one denomination to support a building. The alternative was dedication of religious "Pantheons" for all groups. Lacking a union edifice, worshippers congregated in a store or saloon loaned for the purpose. In the Tootle, Leach & Co. store *(rear, center)* Bishop Daniel Tuttle held the first religious service in Virginia City, Montana.

THE BISHOP IS COMING *(on facing page)*

Religion was one of the earliest cultural importations to the West. Preachers sometimes accompanied wagon trains, and on Sunday the Gospel would be heard. There were never enough ministers to reach all the disconnected mining camps and settlements on the frontier, and the coming of an itinerant man of God was an event as important as the arrival of a supply train or variety troupe. The inhabitants of Wallace, Idaho, welcomed Bishop Ethelbert Talbot to their midst with a broadside.

FIRST CHURCH

In larger western communities, individual denominations felt strong enough to build their own churches. Subscriptions were solicited from everyone, regardless of creed, for a church was a "good thing" to have in town. The Presbyterians of Moorhead, Minnesota built a church *(above)* in the early 1870's. It was used by various denominations until destroyed by fire in 1877.

A RUBE OF THE RUBES (on facing page, bottom)

Among western-born revivalists, best known was William Ashley Sunday, orphaned by the Civil War. Billy had worldly talents. As a boy he won three dollars at a Fourth of July footrace in Ames, Iowa. He played professional baseball for the Chicago White Stockings. But he hit the sawdust trail in 1887 after listening to a group of singers from the Pacific Garden Rescue Mission. "I was born and bred in old Iowa," said Billy later, "I am a Rube of the Rubes, a hayseed of the hayseeds . . . and I expect to go to heaven just the same."

(The Chicago White Stockings, 1886. *Upper:* George Gore, Frank Flint, A. C. Anson, James McCormick, M. J. Kelly, Fred Pfeffer. *Lower:* Unidentified man, Ed. Williamson, Abner Dalrymple, Thomas Burns, John G. Clarkson, William Sunday.)

A GOOD WHOOPIN'

The camp meeting, or revival, successful in eastern states, was introduced to the western country. This type of religious service required no building, and had an emotional and dramatic appeal calculated to stir the hearts of men and women whose relationships with God were casual. At the revival service *(above)* "was unfurled the bloodstained banner of the Red-Shield Cross, bearing for its inscription, 'Holiness to the Lord.'" Converts came to the altar under emotional stress, and, as Father James Rector said to one of them, "It's good for you, you need a good whoopin'."

SAINTS REST

The West offered refuge to the most remarkable religious group ever to form in the United States. To the valley of Salt Lake came the disciples of Joseph Smith, fleeing gentile persecution. In the desert they built a civilization devoted to cooperative, peaceful enterprise, and a Tabernacle *(above)* for the worship of God as interpreted by their prophets.

RELIGION ON THE RESERVATION

The natives of the West were not neglected by those who spread white culture. Religious and educational work among the Indians was simplified by the reservation system. Certain reserves were allotted to one or two denominations by government fiat. Bishop Charles J. O'Reilly *(above)* visits his charges on the Umatilla Reservation.

BILL THE HEALER

Combinations of Christianity and Indian mythology sometimes produced odd results, but religious deviation was not confined to Indians. The Bulgarian Monk of Bay Horse, Idaho, dressed in apostolic robes, pronounced jeremiads over the wicked miners during occasional descents from the hills. Bill the Healer (left) who spent some time in Laramie, Wyoming, was adept in the art of laying on of hands. Bill's hands strayed, and he departed.

FREE LOVER

More widely accepted than stray prophets were the phrenologists who travelled through western settlements reading heads and teaching their art to local enthusiasts. Dr. C. H. DeWolf (right) combined phrenology and free love. The latter phase of his career was terminated by a Washington Territory judge who asked DeWolf and the lady if they regarded themselves as married. "We do," they said. "Well then," said the judge, "by virtue of the powers vested in me by the Territory, I pronounce you man and wife." Appeal was denied.

CHRISTIAN ENDEAVOR

The churches contributed much to the social life of the settlers. Congregations supported and encouraged temperance organizations, and mission societies. Such groups met to transact necessary business, and then bound the ties of Christian love more firmly. The Christian Endeavor society was a popular center of social and cultural activity. Outings of this society *(above)* included not only food and fun, but psalms, hymns, and spiritual songs.

COUNTRY SCHOOL *(on facing page, top)*

The western emigrant, whatever his religious state, was likely to have a high regard for education. School books were recommended as important baggage for emigrants with children. Parents expected to teach their children until schools could be established. The lack of books and teachers was a chronic problem. Public education depended on community cooperation and enterprise, two variables in time and place. Early schools were often one-room shacks attended spasmodically, and supported grudgingly. Teachers were itinerant, poorly paid, and usually ill-trained.

LITTLE GREEN SCHOOLHOUSE *(on facing page, bottom)*

On the plains, school architecture was a practical affair. The settlers lived in sod houses, and their schools were of the same material. In spring, sod schools sprouted greenery. The children who attended this Nebraska school were likely to amount to something in life. They attended out of choice, not necessity. The teachers, often young ladies fresh out of "Institutes," had no tenure; they usually married before tenure became interesting.

120

DISCIPLINE

The problem of keeping frontier schoolchildren under control was much the same as elsewhere. Use of the rod was considered natural and necessary. However, outraged parents could react to real or fancied mistreatment of their offspring. The letter *(right)* was written to a gradeschool teacher in 1864.

PUBLIC EDUCATION

Public-supported schooling of every child gradually gained favor in the West, and territories set up systems of education. Creditable school buildings were erected. The school at Fargo, Dakota *(below)*, was the pride of the town in 1878.

SOUND MINDS

School interiors also improved. The whipsawed plank benches of pioneer days gave way to standard seats, approved by eastern educational theory. The curriculum was enlarged and standardized. Teachers were certified. Mass education had begun.

SOUND BODIES

New educational theories and methods were introduced to the West. Children were subjected to physical training by means of organized play, "wand exercises" *(above)* and similar devices. Such "frills" were especially dear to teachers in city school systems, where drills with wands and dumb-bells were expected to "dispense with pale faces and contracted chests so common in schools."

UMPQUA ACADEMY.

THE fourth quarter of School for the present Academic

year at this Institution, for the year 1860, commenced on MONDAY, JUNE 18.

Winter Term will commence Nov. 1. 1860

REV. T. F. ROYAL, - - - - **Principal.**
MISS C. S. GRUBBE, - - - **Assistant.**
MRS. M. C. DILLON, Teacher of French and Music.

" Mary Clinkinbeard " " "
" My. J. Miller " " "

Rates Reduced:

Primary Classes, per Term of 11 Weeks, . . . $5 00   Music, instrumental, per Term of 11 Weeks, . $8 00
Common English   "   "   "   " . . . 6 00   Incidental Expenses,   "   "   "   " 50al 00
Higher   "   "   "   "   " . . . 7 00   Daily Lessons in Vocal Music, ... *Free.*
Languages, extra,   "   "   "   " . . . 3 00   Good Board can be obtained for $3 00 per week.

No ambitious persons desiring an education shall be

refused a seat in this School for want of means to pay tuition.   Special attention will be paid to book keeping.

No School in Oregon is more favorably situated than

this for health and good morals; and no pains will be spared to render entire satisfaction to those who may patronize it.

BOARD OF TRUSTEES :—Rev. Wm. Miller, Pres't; B. J. Grubbe, John Kuykendall, F. R. Hill, E. Otey, Jas. McKinney, Rev. John Dillard.

HIGHER EDUCATION

Higher education in the West was respected, but impractical. Among the early forms were the "Academies," little more than grade schools, often established by religious groups. Umpqua Academy, a Methodist institution established in 1855, began with a building 30x40 feet, one story, with a second projected. It was, said its founder, "emphatically in a new place—midway between Portland and Yreka." The Academy published catalogues of praiseworthy brevity in broadside form *(above)*.

GRADUATION *(on facing page, top)*

Female academies, devoted to teaching the arts of hemstitching, needlework, and refined manners, were also founded by religious bodies, though attended by all who could find time and tuition. Graduation from such centers of culture involved white dresses, declamations, orations, hearts and flowers.

CHAUTAUQUA *(on facing page, bottom)*

Some westerners with a longing for culture shaved their foreheads so as to look intellectual. Others participated in local debating societies, and lyceums. Efforts toward adult education culminated in the Chautauqua, begun in 1874 as a "Sunday School Teachers' Assembly." Towns prided themselves on Chautauqua halls. The circuit, or tent Chautauqua, which brought culture into every western community, was devised by J. Roy Ellison, born in a Nebraska sod house. The Chautauqua specialized in lectures on temperance, literature, "the battle of life," and similar elevating subjects.

17

It contains the names of thousands of travelers
& Gold hunters 14th went up to Devils
Gate Could not Cross Sweet water Come
Back to the Rock Crosed on a toll bridge
& Come up again to the Devils gate
7 m 15th Travelled up Sweet water
10 m passed the Pound Gap where the
Denver Road Comes in Come 8 m &
Encamped on the River Swam our Stock
over & back for grass 16th Started Early
Come 6 m Met a Company of Soldiers
Stoped for grass then come 11 m further
Pasd the three Crosings come through
Bad Sand 17 come in sight of the
first Snow on the Mountains pased
Ice Springs had a cold Rain &
hail 17 of July & nearly froze with
our Overcoats on drove 20 m without
grass Camped on Sweet water 18th
Forded Sweet water & come 5 m
for dinner Come 6 m to 61

18

South Pass City this afternoon I was
taken sick bones ached head ached
thought I was going to have the
Mountain Fever 19th our Stock started
to Stampede last night but we Staped
them drove 11 m & one of our men
Saw 50 Indians 20th Sunday layed by
21st Come to Sweet water had an Introd
uction to Old Bridger he gave us a
description of the Road to Ft Hall via
of Larders Cut off come 12 m fell in
with & formed into a Company of
16 waggons with a Denver Comp
any we Number about 35 men Elected
William Jack Captain Come along
the base of the Wind River Mts
I went hunting & got sick
22d Come 8 m Crosed the last Crosing
of Sweet water are now going through
the Great South Pass at

LITERARY INDUSTRIES

The condition of education on the frontier was reflected in the lack of home-grown literary talent. The first good writing was produced unwittingly by the overlanders who kept journals or diaries of their experiences. Many such accounts were kept for remembrance' sake; their literary and historical values were discovered by a later generation.

GRASS ROOTS POETRY

For some reason, the emigrants who had a literary urge turned to poetry. Perhaps they felt that poetry could easily be distinguished from prose. Whatever the reason, frontier newspapers were infested with poets who sprang from the sod. The earliest literary publication of the Dakota Territory is the "Ballad of Love's Independence" *(right)*, published in broadside at Fort Rice, and written by Sergeant P. A. Morgan.

BALLAD OF LOVE'S INDEPENDENCE.

When traveling on the waters deep
Sweet thoughts I think of thee,
Sweet Jinnie is the flower for me,
Though far away I am.

One hour is long, the day is longer,
Still further from thee I roam,
And when I lie down at night
I reflect back on thee.

But now we are miles apart,
Let that not grieve your mind,
For when this war is over, dear,
To you I'll return again.

Many miles from you I've roamed,
It was duty called me to go,
While sailing in my boat I thought
Of thee I left behind me.

Nothing have I to cheer my mind,
But thoughts back to thee do soar,
To think I had to part with thee
My heart is filled with pain.

When rolling on the waters deep
The nights are dark and lonesome,
Dear Jinnie, dear, may I be spared
To meet with you once more.

Oh I shall trust in thee, my God,
For all I want to be filled,
For He is the maker and finisher
Of both Heaven and Earth.

The evening I left you, Jinnie,
I felt as though I was lost,

My troubled heart did beat
With tears flowed mingled down.

Now while sailing on my boat,
Oh it is thee I think of,
When rolling on, every minute
My recollection 'tis of thee.

Now further from thee I roam,
Oh may my boat be steered aright,
May it run safe to the shore,
And may I see you once more.

Oh I was once with thee I loved
Who was most precious dear,
Nothing have I now more
To cheer my troubled mind.

If I die far from thee, my love,
Oh bury me between a turtle-dove
To show to your dearest love,
In years to come I died for love.

Forget you not, I'll forget you never,
Till yonder sun goes down forever.
Remember well, and bear in mind
A trusty friend is hard to find.

Oh may all my wants be supplied,
And all my sins be pardoned with God,
Oh may you walk in fear of Him,
And all your relatives follow you.

SERGT. P. A. MORGAN,

Co. E, 1st U. S. V. INF.

POET OF THE SIERRAS

One of the few western poets to gain international acclaim was Cincinnatus H. Miller of Indiana and Oregon. Miller's home folks rated him low as a poet, and even lower as a wife-deserter. But his flowing costume, and sage-brush verse created a stir in the drawing rooms of the East, and salons of England. Joaquin, as he styled himself, was a press-agent, and his fame is in great measure a tribute to the job he did on his only client.

WYOMING AESTHETE

Bill Nye *(right)*, western humorist, came to Wyoming in 1876 with thirty-five cents in his pockets. He undertook several offices and jobs, including justice of the peace, United States Commissioner, postmaster, editor, and staff correspondent for regional newspapers. When Oscar Wilde, en route to San Francisco, stepped off the train at Laramie for a breath of air and an interview, the editor met him at the station. "We told him our name was Nye, the great Wyoming aesthete."

INDIAN POET

Sitting Bull, Sioux medicine man, had, in some circles, the reputation of a considerable poet. The "Works of Sitting Bull," published in Omaha and Chicago under the able editorship of Lt. Robert D. Clarke, went through two editions in their original French, German, and Latin. According to the introduction, S. Bull had early in life been a classical scholar at the Sorbonne. The Chief *(above)* is not playing bashful author; he is ignoring the photographer until a suitable fee has been offered.

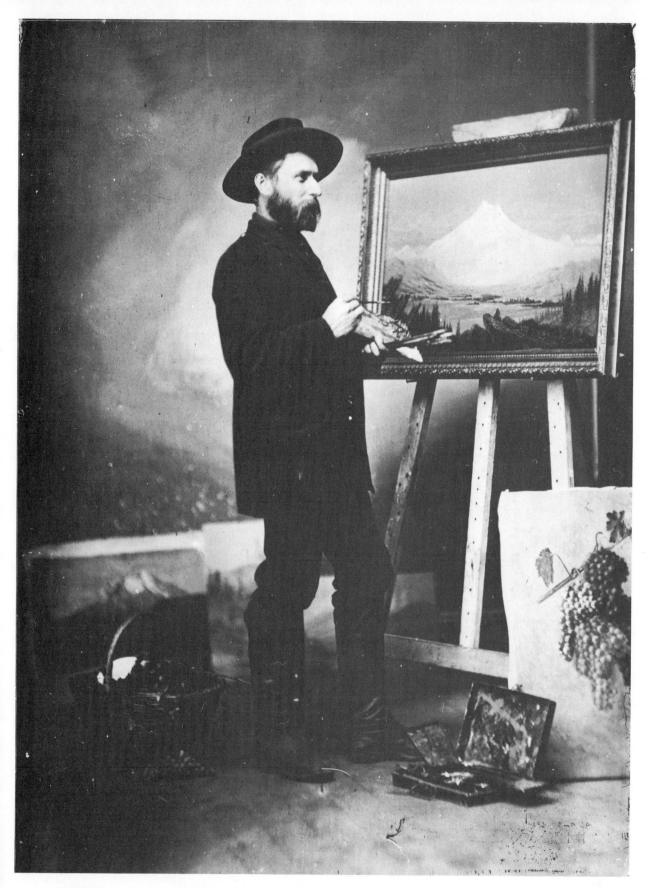

ARTISTS

So far as painters and sculptors were concerned, the western Indians exhibited more talent than the emigrants. Eastern artists were early attracted by the scenic and human values of mountains and plains. The names and reputations of John Mix Stanley and George Catlin are permanently associated with the West. James E. Stuart *(above)*, a native of Maine, studied in San Francisco. He painted western scenery: "Summer Glow, Mt. Takoma," "Sunset Glow, Mt. Hood," "Sunset Glow, Mt. Jefferson," "Sunset, Sacramento." Once Stuart got up early: "Morning, Mt. Hood."

GERMAN BAND

Except for the fiddle at a dance or a melodeon at home, frontier music, in its cultural aspects, was largely confined to amateur bands with plenty of oompah. Carl Klaermer's band *(above)* of Fredericksburg, Texas was German both in style and composition, the town having been settled by German colonists. The musicians were well trained, some of them, no doubt, by Jacob Brodbeck, local music teacher. Brodbeck was a man of parts. He invented an airplane twenty-eight years before the Wright brothers. It was powered by coil spring, and flew to tree-top level. The inventor could never figure a way of rewinding the spring in flight. He went back to music.

CONCERT ENTERTAINERS *(on facing page, top)*

Musical organizations of varying quality travelled through the West from one "booking" to another. The DeMoss Concert Entertainers, a musical family known as the "Lyric Bards," were formed in 1872 by the father, James M., the mother, two sons, and three daughters. The DeMoss quartet, brothers and sisters, travelled throughout the United States, Canada, and Europe, and were Washington, D. C. guests of vice-president Adlai E. Stevenson. At home in eastern Oregon, the family is shown in Yellowstone Park on concert tour.

DOUBLE PLAY

FEATURE of the DeMoss concerts was the playing of George Grant DeMoss, who could dispose of two B♭ cornets in one blow.

THEATER

Of all the arts, theater had probably the greatest popular influence on the frontier. Towns which neglected to provide a church or school took pride in an "Opera House." Much early theater was crude, but the audiences were not especially critical. Variety was to pioneer audiences the spice of theatrical life. McDaniel's New Theatre of Cheyenne offered the miner, Indian fighter, cowhand or floater something to suit every taste.

McDANIEL'S NEW THEATRE

Corner of Sixteenth and Eddy Streets.
CHEYENNE, WYOMING.

J. M. MARTIN .... Director of Amusement
JOS. OLLEREN SHAW .... Leader of Orchestra and Brass Band
WALTER KRIEGER .... Scenic Artist
JOHN SMITH .... Machinist

Entire Change of Programme.

THE CHAMPION VARIETY
THEATRE OF THE WEST!
M'LLE CERITO,
QUEEN OF MAGIC CHANGES
In New Transformations.

THURSDAY EVENING, SEPT. 21, 1876.

Performance will commence with a Grand

Vocal and Instrumental ENTERTAINMENT
By the Ladies and Gentlemen
OF THE COMPANY.

Fancy Dance, - - La Petite Lizzie
Silver Clog, - - Walter Parks
ELLA MARTELL.
Salute La France, - M'lle Aubrey
The Champion Dance,
Master Harry, Summerfield, Parks and Martin.

SELECT BALLADS,
Miss Fannie Garrettson
M'LLE CERITO
IN HER WONDERFUL
TRANSFORMATION DANCES,

The Campaign Orator,
Martin, Parks, Krieger and Summerfield.
When My Ship Comes Home,
Miss Ella Newell.
ELLA MARTELL,
MISS MAGGIE LOUISE.
How About a Room?
Summerfield, Parks, Martin and M'lle Aubrey.
Bouquet of Melodies,
Miss Fannie Garrettson.
Song and Dance, - Maggie Louise
Dolly Day,
MISS ELLA NEWELL.
The Arrival of Bolivar,
Summerfield and Parks.
BALLADS,
Fannie Garrettson.
MAGGIE LOUISE,
All So Happy, - - Ella Newell
To Conclude with
HURRY UP!

ANNOUNCEMENT EXTRAORDINARY!
FRANK AND CARRIE LAVARNIE,
Miss MONTAGUE, and Miss LIZZIE HARMON.
WILL APPEAR SEPT. 25th, 1876.

Grand Balcony Serenade Every Evening by Our Silver Cornet Band.

"LEADER" STEAM BOOK and JOB PRINT, Cheyenne, Wyo.

BERNHARDT VS. HOWE

Established stars took some risks when playing before western audiences. When Sarah Bernhardt *(above)* played *Camille* in Tootle's Opera House, St. Joseph, Missouri, in 1881, the young editor of the Atchison *Globe* was on hand. As Ed Howe saw it, "At exactly 8:31 last night Sarah Bernhardt made her appearance, walking down the centre as though she had but one joint in her body, and no knees. Her dress was of white and costly stuff, and cut so low in front that we expected every moment that she would step one of her legs through it."

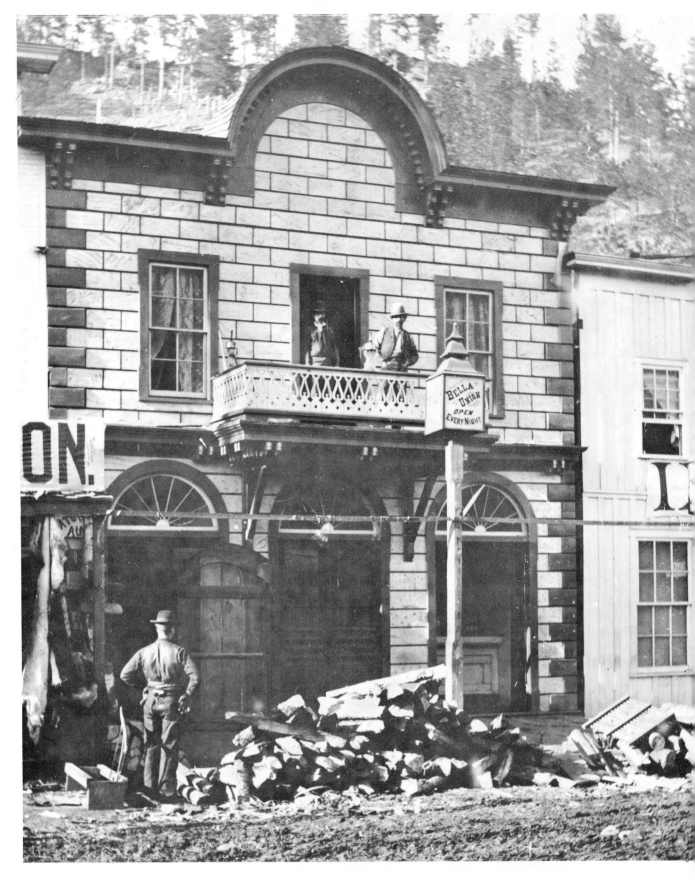

VARIETY

Variety acts appealed to all frontier audiences, and were especially popular in mining towns. The Bella Union (*above*) first theater in Deadwood, was leased in 1876 by Jack Langrishe, he of "long nose and powerful voice." Langrishe specialized in variety. When the show was over, the Bella Union was transformed into a saloon and dance hall. The seventeen curtained boxes were used for the sale of other commodities. If anyone wanted an after-theater snack, the Bella Union was flanked by a lunch counter called "Crumbs of Comfort Along the Crack in the Wall."

ADAH ISAACS MENKEN

The miners of Virginia City, Nevada, were so overwhelmed by the spectacle of Adah Isaacs Menken in pink tights, lashed to a horse, playing *Mazeppa,* they presented her with a $2,000 gold bar.

LITTLE LOTTA

Among the greatest of the stage figures produced in the West was Lotta Crabtree, born in California, and trained by Lola Montez at Grass Valley. Lotta was raised in the tradition of troupers like the George Chapman family, who invented the showboat business on the Mississippi river, and put it on muleback for California miners. Lotta *(below)* first hit the California stage as a child actress. Under the clever management of her mother, she became queen of Variety. Lotta could perform anywhere, from the Bella Union of San Francisco to a redwood stump in the wilds.

PLUSH

The larger western cities prided themselves on fancy theater accommodations. Top-rank performers attracted full houses. Denver's Broadway Theater *(above)* opened August 18, 1890, with the Emma Juch Grand Opera Company playing *Carmen*. The Broadway was said to be the first theater to provide a bathtub in the star's dressing room.

TOPSY'S LAST STAND

Western theater declined as the boom towns faded; only the larger cities remained on the circuit itineraries. The by-ways were served by second-rate troupes doing one-night stands. Old favorites like *Uncle Tom's Cabin (above)* were decorated with extra flourishes to draw a crowd. But the "Opera House" gathered dust most of the year, until the Keystone Cops moved in as permanent replacements for variety and vaudeville.

CHAPTER FIVE

THE MYTH AND ITS MAKERS

BUSY WITH AXE and plough, with the essentials of existence, the western settlers were too preoccupied to produce a written chronicle. Private diaries or letters published in eastern home-town newspapers reflected the genuine pioneer, but popular delineation of the West as a cultural entity was in general left to easterners, to "foreigners" whose approach to the region was in the tradition of American mythology. What had been the Great American Desert became the habitat of western gods and demigods—Jim Bridger for the mountain men, Pecos Bill for the cowboys, Wild Bill Hickok for the gunmen, Buffalo Bill for the nation.

Prototype of the western legend, of the tall tales, the Texas brags, was Colonel Davy Crockett. Like most folk heroes of the West, Crockett was flesh-and-blood transformed. He was a myth even before he died bravely in the Alamo. "I can walk like an ox, run like a fox, swim like an eel, yell like an Indian, fight like a devil, spout like an earthquake, make love like a mad bull, and swallow an Injun whole without choking if you butter his head and pin his ears back."

He was the indestructible westerner, the superman, bragging, brawling, outlandish, the good hero who invariably subdued singlehandedly the vast powers of evil.

For a generation after the Alamo, the mythical Davy Crockett flourished as a folk hero in oral tradition, in newspapers, and in a series of almanacs whose authors were mostly anonymous. The Crockett Almanacs set a pattern for the western myth which was to unfold as a literary form in a flood of dime novels following the Civil War.

While the westerners were pushing toward the beaver country, the mines, and the good land, a young Irishman named Mayne Reid was traveling in western America, living with trappers, hunting buffalo, trading with Indians. After some years of adventure, he visited Philadelphia, became a close friend of Edgar Allen Poe, and decided to try his hand at writing for magazines. Reid was working for Wilkes' *Spirit of the Times* when the Mexican War began. He joined up in 1846, and spent the next three years soldiering and traveling in Mexico and the southwest.

After the war, Mayne Reid settled down in London to begin a thirty-year career of writing adventure novels, most of them based on his exciting decade spent in North America. Reid's plots were rambling and picaresque, but his details of landscape, vegetation, accoutrements and customs were usually exact. He sometimes appended glossaries of western words to his novels. He introduced the treacherous Apache and the mounted horseman with jingling rowels. The speech and dress of his white characters are still used by writers of western fiction, but his Indians all spoke pure Oxford English, and the tribes were often mixed geographically.

In contrast to the Crockett Almanacs' bragging superman, Reid favored an indomitable hero who was usually taciturn, possessed of a mysterious romantic past, and who occasionally bore traces of the medieval knight. During the 1850's and 1860's, Mayne Reid produced a sizable shelf of western American fiction. His works were later reprinted as dime novels and with the tales of James Fenimore Cooper served as prime source books for thousands of paper-backed westerns. By mid-nineteenth century, the eastern public had come to expect certain things from the western scene, and the western myth was rapidly being established.

In 1859, Horace Greeley, editor of the New York *Tribune* made an overland journey to California, enthusiastically reporting everything he saw in the form of letters to his newspaper. At that time Greeley was the most widely read writer in the nation; the weekly edition of his "Try-bune" was a national newspaper, circulating to every village and crossroads. His vivid accounts of the wild West, read eagerly by thousands of subscribers, fixed in the American mind romantic impressions of that far-off land that have not entirely disappeared to this day.

Greeley was too good a newspaperman to disappoint his readers. The western myth, the Crockett flair for exaggeration, struck him as he crossed the Mississippi. "I know that a million buffalo is a great many, but I am certain that I saw that many yesterday." He revived the latent myth of the Great American Desert, placing it between Leavenworth and Denver. (The summer of 1859 *was* hot and dry, and he traveled that section in a slow-moving stagecoach.) And he could not resist adding his bit to the legend of continuous gunfire in western saloons. The gamblers, he said, "had a careless way, when drunk, of firing revolvers, sometimes at each other, and other times quite miscellaneously."

Perhaps the most permanent contribution made by Horace Greeley to the western legend is the story of his ride with Hank Monk who has become the symbol of the speedy stagecoach driver who always brought his passengers through on time. Mark Twain recorded the incident in *Roughing It*: "Drivers always told it, conductors told it, chance passengers told it . . . I never smelt any anecdote so often as I smelt that . . . When Greeley was leaving Carson City he told Hank that he had an engagement that afternoon at Placerville and was anxious to go through quick. Hank cracked his whip and started off at an awful pace. The coach bounced up and down in such a terrific way that it jolted the buttons all off Greeley's coat, and finally shot his head clear through the roof of the stage. He yelled at Hank to go easier—said he wasn't in as much of a hurry as he had thought. But Hank stuck to his first orders. 'Keep your seat, Horace,' he said reassuringly, 'keep your seat and I'll get you there on time!'—and you bet he did, too—what was left of him."

In the autumn of 1860, Americans in some eastern areas were puzzled to find a mysterious advertisement in their newspapers, on signboards, on barn walls, and on sidewalks: "Who is Seth Jones?" A few days later the question was answered with the publication of a dime novel, *Seth Jones; or, The Captives of the Frontier*. Thus appeared the first successful dime novel depicting the frontiersman as hero. *Seth Jones* sold half a million copies, and for a generation appeared in various reprints. It convinced Beadle & Company, the publishers, that "a new mine had been opened."

Edward Sylvester Ellis, author of *Seth Jones*, was a twenty-year-old schoolteacher who had lived most of his life in New Jersey. Offered a contract to write four similar dime novels a year, Ellis fulfilled it in a few days, and began writing other stories under fifteen different pseudonyms. For thirty years he spun out millions of words of western mythology for millions of entranced and credulous readers.

The West's paramount flesh-and-blood folk hero began his astounding literary career without fanfare, December 23, 1869, in Street and Smith's *New York Weekly*. Creator of Buffalo Bill was Edward Z. C. Judson, a veteran author of yellow-backed novels who wrote under the pen name of Ned Buntline. Unlike most dime novel writers, Judson traveled widely, basing his tales upon actual events and persons. He met William Frederick Cody by chance while touring the west in search of story material. Three years after the appearance of *Buffalo Bill, the King of the Border Men*, Judson persuaded Cody to visit New York and act in a stage play. Within a short time Buffalo Bill was permanently established as king of the gods in the mythology of the West.

The legend of Buffalo Bill, though aided by his Wild West Show, was best sustained by Colonel Prentiss Ingraham who took over where Judson left off. Ingraham invented legends about Cody while acting as advance agent for the show, and between 1870 and 1900 he published at least eighty different Buffalo Bill dime novels, most of which were reprinted year after year. Few Americans of that era escaped reading at least one of them, and many undoubtedly accepted the West as a place of pure melodrama with Buffalo Bill the imperishable hero.

It was not only easterners who read and believed. San Francisco's flourishing book stores of that period kept large stocks of western yellow-backs, and the pioneers who crossed the plains read them as they rode. "This wagon," recorded Thomas Creigh, overlander of 1866, "is termed the 'Reading Room,' having no small number of 'Beadles' and other interesting reading matter."

While dime novel authors were writing endless pages of manufactured romance, a modest Texan, John C. Duval, proved with one little book that a straightforward account of a real western hero could be as exciting as a synthetic one. In 1870, Duval published his *Adventures of Big-Foot Wallace, the Texas Ranger and Hunter*. Big-Foot and the Rangers were so popular that a publisher in the East reprinted the book a few months later; it has since gone through seven editions and is still in print.

Although John Duval peopled his story with stock characters—black-souled Mexicans, virtuous maidens, indefatigable heroes—he knew his country and depicted it faithfully. His Indians, mustangs, buffalo, and rattlesnakes were more real than anything Americans could find in their dime novels. "I did not think I was capable of writing a book like those of Mayne Reid," said Duval afterward. "But my young friends said that boys didn't care much for style or literary merit, that all they wanted was a truthful account of scenes and incidents that had actually occurred, not fictitious ones that never had an existence except in the imagination of the author."

After the fashion of Duval, western writers began to base their characters on living persons, some of whose real exploits were being recorded contemporaneously in the press. Actual events in the lives of Kit Carson, Wild Bill Hickok, California Joe, Joaquin Murietta, Billy the Kid and many other western gods and demigods furnished departure points for wild plotting and violent action. A friend once showed Kit Carson the cover of a dime novel which pictured the plainsman slaying seven Indians with one hand while he clasped a fainting maiden with the other. The old scout studied the lurid cover through his spectacles for a long time, finally drawling, "That there may have happened, but I ain't got no recollection of it."

Readers of popular western literature could never be sure which of their heroes were real and which invented. Deadwood Dick became an object of serious tourist search in Deadwood, South Dakota, and the Chamber of Commerce decided to resurrect the popular myth. They selected a long-haired, loquacious old rascal named Dick Clarke to play the role. He proved to be as good a story teller as Edward L. Wheeler, creator of the Deadwood Dick novels. Clarke improved on the history of Custer's Last Stand. He also sold locks of his hair to women tourists, rusty rifles and pistols to the men, and photographs of himself to everybody.

On higher levels of literature the western myth was also in creation. Like a strong breeze out of the West came Mark Twain with his *Celebrated Jumping Frog of Calaveras County* and *Roughing It*. Americans who had laughed over the Crockett Almanacs could laugh again, for here in a wild western setting was Crockett reborn, the genuine native humor of exaggeration, the tall tales of the frontier. Mark Twain rode his frog around the world, and to millions of his listeners and readers, the American West and those who people it became a boisterous extravaganza, fantastic and superhuman.

Contemporaneous with Mark Twain was another westerner, Bret Harte, whose sentimental harlots and noble gamblers have persisted as lively actors in the continuing legends of the Old West.

By 1876 every American surely must have felt in some degree the presence of that fanciful land of buck-skinned giants somewhere beyond the Mississippi. If there were a few who had somehow escaped the legend, they discovered it dramatically early in the summer of that eventful Centennial year. For it was in June of 1876 that George Armstrong Custer led his Seventh Cavalry to doom along the Little Big Horn, focusing the attention of the world on the American West, its Indians and its cavalrymen.

Before the Last Stand, western cavalrymen had played minor roles in the popular literature of the West. But by the time the newspapers and magazines had told and retold the story of the valiant Seventh Regiment, there was a vast demand for tales in which the cavalryman was hero. None was better suited to fulfill this demand than Captain Charles King, a cavalryman himself, who had participated in that Sioux campaign of 1876. King was exact in his details of action, equipment, terrain and weather, but he loved to spin out tales of young lieutenants fresh from West Point, suffering from mysterious pasts, who blundered and then redeemed themselves by gallant fighting. He included heroines who appeared to be Indians but were not, Irish sergeants who swore and drank heavily but always died bravely on the battlefield. For thirty years Charles King wrote of cavalrymen; his plots and characters are still in use today.

Mythology must have its singers, and the West was no exception. John Wallace Crawford, or Captain Jack the Poet Scout, pre-empted the field while Joaquin Miller was sulking on mountain tops or preening himself in Europe. "Often without the least provocation," Jack once said modestly, "I have been in the habit of reciting my poems and singing my songs whenever I could corral a squad of friends and old comrades possessing vitality enough to survive the affliction." Captain Jack's poems were tearjerkers. He once made Wild Bill Hickok weep, and his poems, *The Burial of Wild Bill* and *Wild Bill's Grave* afterwards made thousands of Americans weep—and turned that tall curly-haired gunman into one of the gods of western mythology.

The cowboy came late into western mythology. As there was no cattle industry until after the Civil War, mid-nineteenth century writers had no sources on which to draw. Thomas Pilgrim, using the pseudonym Arthur Morecamp, published *Live Boys*, an authentic fictionized account of cattle trailing in 1878, but not until 1885 did a real cowboy write a book about his experiences. The author was Charlie Siringo; the book was *A Texas Cow Boy; or, Fifteen Years on the Hurricane Deck of a Spanish Pony*.

Charlie Siringo, born in Texas, was a cowboy by nature, but a writer by chance. "I happened to pick up a small scrap of paper and read: 'To the young man of high aim literature offers big inducements, providing he gets into an untrodden field.'" Siringo decided rightly that cow-punching, the only field he knew, was untrodden. "My excuse for writing this book is money—and lots of it," was his opening sentence. The excuse was valid, for *A Texas Cow Boy* sold close to a million copies. It must have been a rich source book for the dime novel factories, though there was little romance in Siringo's simple telling of his boyhood, of how he went "on a tare" in Wichita, of the Chisholm Trail. He wrote like a cowboy talking. Charlie Siringo proved that folklore is not invented, and that perhaps the western myth was true after all.

The reality of *A Texas Cow Boy* was not to endure. In 1902 *The Virginian* appeared. He and the long line of soft-voiced knights on horseback who succeeded him have since dominated the legend.

"The Virginian's pistol came out, and his hand lay on the table, holding it unaimed. And with a voice as gentle as ever, the voice that sounded almost like a caress, but drawling a very little more than usual, so that there was almost a space between each word, he issued his order to the man Trampas:—"When you call me that, *smile.*"

That is the most famous scene in western fiction, from the book that J. Frank Dobie has called the "classic cowboy novel without cows." The author was Owen Wister, Harvard graduate and Philadelphia lawyer, who went west on a visit for the first time in 1885, the year Charlie Siringo's *A Texas Cow Boy* made its appearance.

The image of the horseman as cavalier had moved across the old South into Texas, and then as the Texas cattlemen went north into Wyoming and Montana to claim the open ranges as feudal barons, they carried with them this vision of knighthood. The ranchers were the last cavaliers, the knights of the range, in strong contrast to the Crockett Almanacs' bumptious vulgarians. Owen Wister no doubt met a few real cowboys, but his associates were in the main wealthy ranch owners, feudal barons derived from Texas or directly from Britain. All around him were cavaliers on horseback wearing chaps instead of armor.

The Virginian became a best-seller immediately, and for the first time a western story achieved respectability. It was bound in cloth, stocked in public libraries, and could be read by Americans openly in family living rooms. Made respectable by *The Virginian,* the western story began to flourish in board covers. Emerson Hough compromised with historical truth for the sake of the myth; Zane Grey averaged almost two titles a year for a generation as a prolific make-believer. A woman, Bertha Muzzy Sinclair, created *Chip of the Flying U* in 1906. Chip and his punchers rode the Montana ranges in book after book, cavorting and conversing with all the good clean fun of the Rover Boys.

Probably the most enduring of all make-believe cowboy folk heroes, Hopalong Cassidy, was born in 1910, the creation of Clarence E. Mulford. Hopalong was Don Quixote played straight, and like some other synthetic western heroes owes his fame more to the moving pictures than to the printed word. For in those innocent buoyant years of the new century, when Americans were reading *The Virginian* and its many imitations, a new invention brought nickelodeons into downtown streets. The makers of these moving pictures quickly discovered that the western scenarios were among the most popular, and to this day one of the axioms of that extraordinary industry is that a "horse opera" rarely loses money.

Like all early moving pictures, the first westerns were simple in plot and characterization, with good and evil in sharp, unreal contrast. In one of these first ventures, *The Life of a Cowboy,* 1906, there are four standard scenes—a bar, a stagecoach, a holdup, and a chase. After half a century the pattern has remained the same.

Real cowboys, of course, rarely ever saw a stagecoach, and when they did the chances of its being held up were remote. They visited saloons much less frequently than New Yorkers, and seldom chased anything more villainous than a bad-tempered steer. But from that day to this the myth has thrived, with shadow heroes subduing evil in a shadow land of gods and demigods, a West the pioneers never knew and probably never imagined in their wildest dreams.

DAVY CROCKETT, RING-TAILED ROARER

Prototype for the western legends, the tall tales and Texas brags, was Colonel Davy Crockett. Like most western folk heroes, Crockett was flesh-and-blood, but he was a myth even before he died bravely in the Alamo. He was the indestructible westerner, the superman—brawling and outlandish—but a good hero who inevitably subdued singlehandedly the vast powers of evil.

MAYNE REID: RIFLE RANGERS AND SCALP HUNTERS

While the western settlers were busy with axe and plough, a young Irishman, Mayne Reid *(left)*, was traveling among them, hunting Buffalo, living with trappers, trading with the Indians. After soldiering with the United States Army in the Mexican War of 1846-48, he settled down in London to begin a thirty-year career of writing novels based on his adventures. Mayne Reid introduced the treacherous Apache and the mounted horseman hero—a hero who was taciturn, possessed of a mysterious past, and who occasionally bore traces of the medieval knight.

HORACE GREELEY GOES WEST

In 1859, Horace Greeley *(right)*, editor of the New York *Tribune* made an overland journey to California, enthusiastically reporting everything he saw. One of the most widely read writers in America at that time, Greeley was too good a newspaperman to disappoint his public. His readers expected a "wild" West, and they got it. Greeley's vivid accounts fixed in the American mind romantic impressions of that far land that have not entirely disappeared to this day. He saw herds of "a million buffalo," he crossed a Great American Desert, he recorded the undying legend of continuous gunfire in western saloons, and he discovered the perfection of California's climate.

HANK MONK, LEGENDARY COACHMAN

One of Greeley's unintentional contributions to the western legend is the story of his ride with Hank Monk, who has become a symbol of the speedy stagecoach driver who always brought his passengers through on time. Recording the event in *Roughing It,* Mark Twain described how all the buttons were jolted off Greeley's coat, how his head crashed through the top of the stage. "Keep your seat, Horace," Hank Monk reassured him, "keep your seat and I'll get you there on time."

BEADLE'S HALF DIME Library

Copyrighted in 1877, by BEADLE AND ADAMS.

| Vol. I. | Single Number. | BEADLE AND ADAMS, PUBLISHERS, No. 98 WILLIAM STREET, NEW YORK. | Price. 5 Cents. | No. 8. |

SETH JONES;
OR,
The Captives of the Frontier.

BY EDWARD S. ELLIS.

CHAPTER I.
THE STRANGER.

THE clear ring of an ax was echoing through the arches of a forest, three-quarters of a century ago; and an athletic man was swinging the instrument, burying its glittering blade deep in the heart of the mighty kings of the wood.

Alfred Haverland was an American, who, a number of years before, had emigrated from the more settled provinces in the East, to this then remote spot in western New York. Here, in the wilderness, he had reared a humble home, and, with his loving partner and a sister, laid the foundation for a settlement. True, this "settlement" was still small, consisting only of the persons mentioned, and a beautiful blue-eyed maiden, their daughter; but Haverland saw that the tide of emigration was rolling rapidly and surely to the west, and, ere many years, that villages and cities would take the place of the wild forest, while the Indians would be driven further on toward the setting sun.

The woodman was a splendid specimen of "nature's noblemen." His heavy coat lay upon a log a short distance away, and his swelling, ponderous chest was covered only by a close-fitting under-garment, with the collar thrown open, showing the glowing neck and heaving breast. Substantial pants met the strong moccasins which incased his feet. A small raccoon-skin cap rested on the back of his head, exposing his forehead, while his black hair swept around his shoulders. His features were regular, and strongly marked. The brow was rather heavy, the nose of the Roman cast, and the eyes of a glittering blackness. So he stood with one foot thrust forward; his muscles, moving and ridging as they were called into play, betrayed their formidable strength.

Still the flashing ax sunk deeper and deeper into the oak's red heart, until it had gone clean through and met the breach upon the opposite side. Then the grand old forest-king began to totter. Haverland stepped back and ran his eyes to the top, as he noticed it yielding. Slowly it leaned, increasing each second, until it rushed seemingly forward, and came down to the earth with a thundering crash and rebound. He stood a moment, his hot breath issuing like steam from his chest, and then moved forward toward its branches. At that instant his trained ear detected a suspicious sound, and, dropping his ax, he caught up his rifle and stood on the defensive.

"How de do? How de do? Ain't frightened, I hope; it's nobody but me, Seth Jones, from New Hampshire," said the new-comer in a peculiar accent. As the woodman looked up he saw a curious specimen of the *genus homo* before him. He is what is termed a *Yankee*, being from New Hampshire; but he was such a person as is rarely met with, and yet which is too often described, nowadays. He possessed a long, thin Roman nose, a small, twinkling gray eye, with a lithe, muscular frame, and long, dangling limbs. His feet were incased

in well-fitting shoes, while the rest of his dress was such as was in vogue on the frontiers at the time of which we write. His voice was in that peculiar, uncertain state, which is sometimes seen when it is said to be "changing." When excited, it made sounds singular and unimaginable.

The woodman, with characteristic penetration, read the man before him at a glance. Changing his rifle to his left hand, he extended the other.

"Certainly not, my friend; but then, you know, these are times in which it behooves us all to use caution and prudence; and where one is placed in such a remote section as this it would be criminal to be careless, when more than one life is dependent upon me for support and protection."

"Very true, very true; you're right there, Mr.—ah! I declare I don't know your name."

"Haverland."

"You're right, as I said, Mr. Have-your-land, or Haverland, as the case may be. I tell *you* these *are* dubious times—no disputin' that, and I was considerably s'prised when I heard the ring of an ax down in these parts."

"And I was equally surprised to meet your visage when I looked up. Jones, I believe you said was your name?"

"Exactly—Seth Jones, from New Hampshire. The Joneses are a numerous family up there—rather too many of them for comfort—so I migrated. Mought be acquainted, perhaps?"

"No, I have no acquaintance to my knowledge in that section."

"Haven't, eh? Thought the Joneses were pretty generally known through the country. Some remarkable geniuses have sprung from the family. But what under the sun keeps you out in this heathen country? What brought you here?"

"Enterprise, sir; I was tired of the civilized portion of our country, and when such glorious fields were offered to the emigrant as are here spread before him, I considered it a duty to avail myself of them, and I have done so. And now, sir, be equally frank with me, and let me know what induced you to visit this perilous region when you had no reason to suppose that a settlement had yet been commenced by the whites. You look to me as if you were an Indian-hunter or scout."

"Wal, perhaps I am. At any rate I have been. I was a scout among the Green Mountain Boys, under Colonel Allen, and stayed with them till the Revolution was finished. After that I went down on the farm and worked a while with the old man. Something occurred in our neighborhood that kill me to think it was best for me to leave; I won't say what it was, but I will say it was no crime I committed. I stopped at the settlement down the river a few days, and then come to the conclusion to take a tramp in these parts."

"I am very glad you have come, for it isn't often we get sight of a white face. I hope you will take the welcome of a backwoodsman, and make your home with us as long a time as you can —remembering that the longer you stay the more welcome you will be."

"I shall probably stay till you git tired of me, at any rate," laughed the eccentric Seth Jones.

"As you are from the East, probably you can give information of the state of feeling among the Indians between that section and us. From your remarks, I should infer, however, that nothing very serious threatens."

"Don't know 'bout that," replied Seth, shaking his head and looking to the ground.

"Why so, my friend?"

"I tell you what, you, I heerd orful stories long the way. They say since this war, the darned red-coats have kept the Injins at work. Leastways, it's pretty sartin they are at work, anyhow."

"Are you sure?" asked the woodman, betraying an anxiety in his speech.

"Purty sure. There's a little settlement down here some miles, (I forgot the name,) not on by the imps and burned all up."

"Is it possible? Reports have reached me during the past three or four months of the deadly hostility existing between the whites and reds, but I was glad to doubt it. Although I sometimes felt it was wrong."

"'Twas so; and if you vally that air wife of your busum, and your little cherubims, (as I allow you've got,) you'd better be makin' tracks for safer quarters. Why, how have you stood it so long?"

"My conduct toward the Indians has ever been characterized by honesty and good-will upon my part, and they have ever evinced a friendly feeling toward me and my helpless ones. I place great reliance upon this state of feeling, in fact, my only reliance."

SETH JONES.

THE CREATION OF BUFFALO BILL

The West's paramount flesh-and-blood hero began his literary career without fanfare, December 23, 1869, in Street & Smith's *New York Weekly*. Creator of Buffalo Bill was Edward Z. C. Judson, veteran author of yellow-backed novels, who used the pseudonym Ned Buntline. Judson had met William Frederick Cody while traveling in the West. After the success of *King of the Border Men,* Cody visited New York to act in a stage play. Within a short time, Buffalo Bill was established as king of the gods in the mythology of the American West.

PRENTISS INGRAHAM: EIGHTY BUFFALO BILLS

Buffalo Bill furthered his legend by traveling the world with his Wild West Show, but the man who kept it burning brightly was Colonel Prentiss Ingraham *(left)*. Between 1870 and 1900 Ingraham published at least eighty different Buffalo Bill dime novels. He obtained his material first hand, traveling with Cody in the West and sometimes acting as advance agent for the show.

WILLIAM (BIG FOOT) WALLACE

While dime novel authors were writing millions of words of manufactured western romance, a modest Texan named John C. Duval proved that a true account of a real western hero could be more exciting than invented exploits of imaginary characters. In his *Adventures of Big Foot Wallace*, Duval presented to the world the glamorous Texas Rangers and the story of William A. Wallace (shown at *right*).

"*On with the dance; Let joy be unconfined!*"

GRAND NEW YEAR'S BALL,

—AT THE—

"OSAGE VALLEY HOUSE"

OSAWATOMIE, K. T.,

FRIDAY, DECEMBER 30, 1859.

Your Company is Respectfully Solicited.

COMMITTEE OF INVITATION.

V. I. WILLS, Osawatomie.	B. F. SIMPSON, Paola.
L. C. CRITTENDEN, "	WM. CROWELL, "
ED. YOUMANS, Indianapolis.	A. B. SQUIRES, Squiresville.
WM. A. MOSLEY, Miami.	D. B. MITCHELL, Paris.
WM. NICHOLS, Stanton.	C. R. JENISON, Mound City.

FLOOR MANAGERS.

R. W. WOOD, H. B. SMITH.

GOOD MUSIC WILL BE IN ATTENDANCE.

SUPPER AT TEN O'CLOCK.

BILL, $2,50.

FISHER & CROUCH, Proprietors.

ON WITH THE DANCE

When the western emigrant wanted some jollification, the fiddle "at early candle lightin'" was usually handy. Little planning, a minimum of equipment, and much energy was all it took to enjoy this form of frontier entertainment.

LIGHT FANTASTIC TOE

"Methodist feet" was an affliction that troubled few persons when a social was in progress. Dances were held on the slightest provocation, or on none at all. In frontier society where women were scarce, men organized stag dances, either with designated partners, or on a solo basis. River raftsmen *(above)* were noted for their fiddling and prancing. Lewis and Clark's boatmen danced for the edification of the Indians.

LIGHT AND TIE

Just "visiting" was a popular means of fron entertainment (above). A visit might last a or a long week-end. It meant news, exchang gossip, interruption of routine, and a brea the loneliness of thinly settled areas. Hospit was rewarding, and prompt. As one visitor scribed his welcome, "The lady of the h kicked the dogs out of the corner by the fire, some pieces of fat side meat, made corn dod and strong coffee. She said she had no sas give us but tongue sass, as there was no hole."

THE DAY WE CELEBRATE

The Fourth of July was the most commonly vigorously celebrated of all western holic Originally confined to joy-shooting, speed and much drinking, the order of events grad expanded to include a maximum of commu participation, noise, and patriotic fervor. broadside illustrates an obsolete feature of I pendence Day celebrations, the mock parad masked celebrators, the "Ancients and ribles," held before the evening ceremonies.

GRAND PROCESSION

The parade was the big whoop-up event of the Fourth of July. Patriotic and military organizations dominated the affair, but decorated floats sponsored by merchants, fraternal organizations, or churches provided opportunity for all to participate. The fire department of Henderson, Minnesota *(above)*, is followed by marching members of the Grand Army of the Republic on July 4, 1893.

FRIENDS . . . AND VOTERS

"The small boy's paradise, and the politician's opportunity," Independence Day was littered with fragments of firecrackers and political oratory. "Patriotism, pie-ty, roast beef and cakes," commented one young man, "I saw a great variety of slim-legged girls."

PLAY BALL!

When baseball became popular after the Civil War, Fourth of July festivities usually included an afternoon game between local teams. In the 1880's it took seven bad pitches to walk a man, and the batter could call for a high or low pitch, as he pleased. The Pendleton and Arlington teams of 1886 *(above)* were recruited from the wheat fields of eastern Oregon. For speedier base running they took off their shoes.

ON THE MARK! *(on facing page, top)*

The westerners made games of their occupational skills. Volunteer firemen were proud of the speed of their companies, and challenged other outfits to contests. Tournaments between towns, and even between states decided champions. The Eastern Oregon and Washington fireman's tournament held in 1896, was a major event. The 220-yard dash over the dirt streets of Pendleton was won by King Witt *(fourth from left)* in 24⅕ seconds.

HOOK AND LADDER RACE *(on facing page, bottom)*

Firemen's tournaments included tests of speed with equipment. The hook and ladder company pulled its gear from a standing start to a given point, usually one hundred yards away, raised the ladder to maximum height, and placed a man on the top rung. In the tournament the Pendleton lads performed the operation in 28⅖ seconds.

"WE HAVE BECOME A RACE OF MERCURYS"

The bicycle provided recreation for townspeople. The first bicycle was introduced in America in 1876. In four years the sport had become so popular that a League of American Wheelmen was formed "to promote the general interests of bicycling, to ascertain, protect, and defend the rights of wheelmen, and to encourage and facilitate touring." The League also established rules for racing. The starters (*above*) are waiting at a meet of Twin City Wheelmen, 1891.

MINERS' CONTEST (*on facing page, top*)

In mining districts where hardrock work and blasting were necessary skills, miners staged rock drilling contests. Cooperation between the man with the sledge and the man with the drill required an acute sense of timing, and mutual trust.

BIRLING (*on facing page, bottom*)

Of the many skills required of a logger, most spectacular was his ability to ride logs through swift water, and handle himself on a slippery stick. Contests between loggers were based on ability to balance, while throwing off an opponent. In some regions, birling contests were advertised as an annual attraction, and drew contestants out of the woods from surrounding states. Such affairs ended in celebrations of mutual friendship at which water was notably absent.

KOSTOMLOTSKY OF OSKALOOSA

Racers, decided the League of American Wheelmen, "must wear shirts that shall not bare the shoulders, and breeches that must reach the knee." Clothed in official decorum, cyclists competed at various distances, and in trick riding. Emil Kostomlotsky *(above)* of Oskaloosa, Iowa, was a great local favorite.

GENTEEL EXERCISE

The ladies, too, in proper wheeling habit, were encouraged to cycle for reasons of health. A physician of the time, called on to comment on the "bicycle craze" as it affected women argued that "the lower extremity of the human female has great latent possibilities." Mrs. John Gazette (*above*) of Rice, Minnesota, sets out with a group of friends.

IMPROVING THE BREED

The condition of most western roads made bicycling difficult. Horse racing did not require smooth courses, and was a sport that appealed in country where almost every man owned or could borrow a mount. In the absence of a track, horse races were run down Main Street. Much money changed hands at such events, especially when a local favorite was left behind by a trained runner introduced by gypsy horse traffickers.

WINTER SPORTS

Among the earliest western winter sports were the "sliding clubs," formed about 1864 in the mountain towns of Idaho. Such contests, "unobjectionable from a moral standpoint," involved racing with cutters down snow-covered hills. Stakes for a grand race between towns ran as high as $2,500. Ski clubs, too, were formed in mountain states. Called "snow-shoers," the clubs engaged in cross-country jaunts, rather than down-hill races. The snow-shoers of Gunnison, Colorado (above), were active in 1883.

RANCH TRACK

Wealthy ranchers interested in horse racing built their own tracks, established local rules, and in general took the sport seriously. The enclosed mile track *(above)* at the Daly ranch near Helena, Montana, was a headquarters for local horse fanciers. Here both ranch ponies and racing stock provided entertainment.

"GAME IS PLENTIFUL JUST NOW"

Not all frontier amusements depended on competition in the useful arts, or the attractions of outdoor exercise. "Game," said one observer, "is plentiful just now. Buffalo, draw poker, antelope, old sledge. . . ." Few pastimes were simpler, more congenial, and to some more profitable, than a card game. Where money was plentiful, the stakes in a poker game were high; if cash was not on hand, gold dust, mining claims, and sometimes Indian concubines changed hands.

FAMILY FUN

While the rougher element was exchanging money across the poker tables, the average settler found joy in the simple life. Strawberry festivals were a familiar entertainment among town and country folks alike. Everyone enjoyed eating, and the festival advertised the agricultural qualities of a community. The festival at Glenwood, Colorado *(above)*, was sponsored by the Midland Railroad, interested in attracting settlers.

BLANKET DICE *(on facing page, top)*

Noted for gambling were the cowboys. In lieu of formal saloon equipment, cowhands spread a blanket on the prairie, and shot craps. Horse and saddle were sometimes lost in a few throws. The cowhands shown are rolling a few on the JA ranch, in Texas. The white-shirted tenderfoot on the right is George Patullo, short-story writer from the East, friend of the photographer, Erwin E. Smith.

GAMBLING JOINT *(on facing page, bottom)*

For westerners who required organized entertainment, the saloon and gambling house was readily available. Here a man could lose his pile over poker, euchre, faro, billiards, or on a wager concerning the exact arrival time of the next stage. Gambling houses were constant targets of moral objection, and the Denver city council at one time outlawed three-card monte, but conveniently neglected to ban other games of skill. The Sheridan House bar and billiard room, Bismarck, Dakota, was a friendly spot in 1879.

PICNIC

The Sunday School picnic was another approved form of entertainment. Held annually, it offered plenty of food, lemonade, unexceptionable atmosphere, and sports of the jolly sort, including sack races *(above)*.

SPARKING SCHOOLS

Singing schools were also regarded as improving for the young. Supposed to be a cultural activity, the singing school was referred to by participants as a "sparking school." The real activity of the evening commenced when couples strolled quietly home after an evening of music and song. The singing school *(above)* flourished in 1866.

THE SURROUND

Early western settlers found every opportunity to make a game of work. If a job was too large for one man, he invited his neighbors to help. House-raising and barn-raising were jobs which drew neighborly assistance from miles around. Less known, though more spectacular, were the rabbit drives, community projects carried on as sport. They were necessary where jackrabbits were a menace to haystacks. Corral and wings were constructed, and the drive was on. Settlers turned out on horseback and on foot to join the fun.

THE KILL

Once the drive was over, men armed with clubs and cleavers entered the corral and beat the varmints to death. "Lunch would then be served, and a good time was had by everyone." Control of jackrabbits became scientific when agricultural colleges took to germ warfare, and successfully planted a fatal disease among the rabbit population of some western states.

MEAT HUNTER

Hunting was one of the most practical and generally enjoyed western sports. The plains were the last stand of big game in the United States, personified by the American bison. By 1882, when this picture was taken, buffalo hunting was restricted to a few areas in Montana.

ROYAL HUNTER

Only ten years before, buffalo roamed the plains of Nebraska. In January, 1872, Grand Duke Alexis of Russia was entertained with a big-game hunt supervised by General Sheridan. Buffalo Bill was on hand as chief guide. The Grand Duke, dressed in jacket and trousers of heavy gray cloth, trimmed with green, and buttons bearing the imperial Russian coat of arms, got his buffalo. As added entertainment, Spotted Tail and a band of Brule Sioux were gathered to demonstrate Indian skill in bow and arrow hunting. General Custer was of course on hand, "resplendent in his flowing hair and foppish military dress."
(Left to right, front: Gen. J. W. Forsyth, Lt. Stordegraff, Col. M. V. Sheridan. *Center:* Consul Bodisco, Chancellor Machen, Lt. Gen. P. H. Sheridan, Grand Duke Alexis, Admiral Possiet, Gen. G. A. Custer. *Rear:* Frank Thompson, Doctor Kadrin, Col. George A. Forsyth, Count Olsonfieff, Dr. Morris J. Asch, Gen. Sweitzer, Lt. Tudor.)

PLEASURE HUNTER

Westerners were quick to realize the attractions of the "wild and woolly" for adventure-hunting easterners. Advertisements were circulated urging "pleasure seekers" to join guided expeditions "over the wild prairie for buffalo and antelope." Such sport was made comfortably available by the advance of railroads across the hunting grounds. The Jerome Marble and Henry Houghton party *(above)* of Worcester, Massachusetts, came west in Marble's privately built hunting car in 1876.

EXECUTIVE TOURIST

Not all eastern visitors came to hunt. Some of them just liked the scenery. Among the latter was President Chester A. Arthur, who toured Yellowstone Park in 1883. En route, at Fort Washakie, he was greeted by an Indian council *(above)*. The Indians presented the White Father with a pony for his daughter, little Nell. President Arthur was in good hands; his party included one governor, two generals, two colonels, a captain, a judge, a senator, and one cabinet member.

WESTERN GUIDE

To make sure that President Arthur saw Yellowstone Park in comfort, Chief Packer Tom Moore *(above)* was employed as supply man. Moore had witnessed Indian wars from Oregon to Arizona, had been with George Crook at the battle of the Rosebud in 1876, and had developed the pack train to a high art. Celebrities were no novelty to Moore; in 1880 he had performed as packer for the "spindleshanked Mephistopheles," Secretary of the Interior Carl Schurz, also on a visit to Yellowstone.

ROUGHING IT

After the emigrant had settled his new land and built a comfortable house, he too regarded the mountains and plains as a source of recreation. It seemed fitting to revisit some of the spots which had been passed on the overland trip, and seen hastily from a covered wagon. The pioneer packed his tent and gear, and went to the mountains for fun.

HISTORIC SITE

Historic sites along the western trails were in some instances pre-empted by enterprising business men. Hot springs, in particular, were enclosed, and their waters advertised as healing. Steamboat Springs (*above*) famous in overland literature, was metamorphosed into a bathroom.

GRAND HOTEL

The new western tourist was given the best of care in palatial hotels, established where only flea houses had flourished before. The Broadwater Hotel greeted the tourists of 1890. Attached to the hotel was a hot-springs bath, elegantly camouflaged as a "Natatorium" *(above)*. Helena, Montana, had come a long way.

MOUNTAIN MEADOW

The railroads, too, understood the profit of resort hotels. Glenisle, established in the Platte Canyon, Colorado, was a summer rendezvous for a tired Denver executive, or for an eastern family anxious for a summer in the mountains. The Glenisle golf course *(above)* was the ultimate use for the mountain meadow, a spot once celebrated for its beaver, later for the grass it provided for jaded emigrant ox-teams. The wild West was now civilized.

CHAPTER SEVEN

WILD WEST SHOWS AND RODEOS

IN THEIR SEARCH for jollification, western settlers developed rodeo, an original sport probably more indigenous to this continent than baseball. Rodeo had its simple beginnings in the roundup camps of cowboys, but as an organized sport it was nurtured in the old wild west shows.

The first modern rodeo may have been the rehearsals held at North Platte, Nebraska, in 1883, by Buffalo Bill Cody for his Wild West Show. Cody, who had accumulated several thousand dollars touring with a stage show, advertised throughout the West that he was organizing a company of "cowboys, Mexican vaqueros, famous riders and expert lasso throwers." So many applied for jobs as "actors" that he arranged a roping and riding competition to select the best. Buffalo Bill's Wild West Show opened at the fair grounds in Omaha, May 17, 1883.

Many a western town and city, however, lays claim to the honor of holding the first rodeo. In 1847, Mayne Reid reported that he witnessed a roping contest at Santa Fe. According to newspaper accounts, Cheyenne had some unorganized cowboy contests in 1872. Colorado's state fair of 1876, held in Denver, featured a race between a cowboy and a horse. Winfield, Kansas, claims the first rodeo was an exhibition held there by the 101 Ranch in 1882.

The same summer that Buffalo Bill's Wild West Show took to the road, 1883, the first roping and riding tournament was held in Texas. Some cowboys got into a friendly argument in a Pecos City saloon as to whether the Hashknife, the Mill Iron, or the Lazy Y had the best bronc riders and steer ropers. To settle the argument, they decided to hold a public contest on July 4th. Using the courthouse yard as a corral and Pecos City's main street for an arena, the cowboys put on quite a show.

Rodeo's real origins, of course, were in the roundup camps of the cowboys. Even before the great cattle drives up the Chisholm Trail, vaqueros in Mexico were holding tournaments for the best ropers and riders. It was no accident that the Spanish word for roundup, *rodeo,* came into use early as the name for the most popular sport in the West.

Horse racing was always a favored amusement of westerners. The larger towns and some big ranches had race tracks, but a track was unnecessary if rival range outfits happened to get together and start boasting of the relative speeds of their cow ponies. They raced right off across the prairie. If a high-spirited bronc turned up in a horse herd, an informal riding contest was usually arranged on the spot, the spectators placing bets as to how long each competitor could ride bareback, or in the saddle. And whenever two or more cowboys were otherwise unoccupied for a few minutes, more than likely they would compete with each other at rope-throwing.

For many years, however, these local contests were purely amateur, and if an expert rider or roper wanted to earn money with his special skills he had to join a wild west show. The success of Buffalo Bill's "cowboys, riders and expert lasso throwers" soon brought many imitators into the business. Touring circuses added riding and roping acts, often changed their names to wild west shows. As might have been expected, these shows were quite popular with western settlers; they would travel long distances to see tent shows if there was plenty of roping and riding and shooting guaranteed with each performance.

Some tamed-down western towns that had lived with wild cowboys through trail-driving days were not entirely happy to see them return with the tent shows—especially if the boys slipped from make-believe back to real old-time wildness. The Cheyenne *Democratic-Leader* of July 22, 1884, commented on a visiting show: "Last night at 12 o'clock, cowboys belonging to Hardwick's Wild West Show made a drunken raid on South Clark street in regular western style. They succeeded in frightening the people from the streets, and were finally captured by the police and locked up. Twelve large navy revolvers and a large knife were secured. The entire party was bailed out this morning, and this afternoon gave the usual exhibition to a crowd of 12,000 people. The cowboys in their raid last night where led by Ben Circkle, for years a celebrated character in the far West."

Meanwhile in the southwest, riding and roping contests were continuing to gain popularity. During the summer of 1888, cowboys from the Laurel Leaf Ranch organized a two-day celebration in Canadian, Texas. Horse racing and square-dancing were on the program, but the main event was a steer-roping contest. From miles around, folks rode into Canadian on horseback and in creaking buckboards. Ellison Carroll won the roping contest on that day, and, for the next quarter of a century, he was undisputed king of the steer ropers.

On July 4, 1888, Prescott, Arizona, initiated its famous Frontier Days, including in the celebration what was probably the first commercial rodeo. Winning ropers and riders received small cash prizes, and spectators paid admission fees. For years, Arizonians had been fond of traveling street circuses, *romeriomaras,* which came up from Mexico with clowns and acrobats and trick riders. Arizona also is the only state in the Union which ever supplied camels for a wild west show—nine camels which had escaped from the old

War Department herd imported for desert use before the Civil War. So it is not surprising that Prescott organized the first commercial rodeo.

The hero of that Independence Day of 1888 was a cowboy named Juan Leivas who received a silver trophy inscribed as follows: "Citizens Prize, contested for and won by Juan Leivas over all competitors at the Fourth of July Tournament. Held in Prescott, A. T., 1888. For roping and tieing steer. Time 1:17½, 100 yards start."

In the northwestern range country, the woolly-chapped ropers and riders kept their contests on an amateur basis until 1893. In that year, E. Farlow of Lander, Wyoming, combined a cowboy tournament with a wild west show and circus. Farlow borrowed the Frontier Days idea from Arizona, but he added stagecoach holdups and horse-team relay races to the usual bronco-busting and steer-roping events. Lander's first Frontier Days was a grand show, but spectators were few, consisting mostly of participants relaxing between other contests.

After the slow start of Lander's Frontier Days, rodeo languished in the thinly populated northwest. Contests were held at some of the stockmen's conventions in Montana, and cowboys from some of the larger Wyoming ranches occasionally met for informal rivalry. Then in 1897, Cheyenne staged its first Frontier Days. Cheyenne still considered itself the "cowboy capital," but even so the rodeo organizers sought aid from the Union Pacific Railroad to insure a paying crowd. Special trains brought in thousands of spectators in 1897, and the show was a success, with seats selling at fifteen to thirty-five cents.

Wyoming, the first state to give women the vote, was also the first to admit them to rodeo. The first girl contestant was Bertha Kaepernick, who entered both the bucking contest and the wild horse race staged at Cheyenne's premiere Frontier Days. "She rode a wild horse in front of the grandstand," said Warren Richardson, one of the organizers of the celebration, "and she stayed on him all the time. Part of the time he was up in the air on his hind feet; once he fell backward, and the girl deftly slid to one side only to mount him again as he got up. She rode him in the mud to a finish, and the crowd went wild with enthusiasm."

Cheyenne also borrowed the most popular feature of Buffalo Bill's Wild West Show —a stagecoach holdup. It was a "thrilling event," according to the newspapers, but the stunt which truly gave the customers their money's worth was the hanging of a horse thief by a vigilante posse. Bill Root, Laramie newspaper man, played the part of the horse thief up to the moment when the noose came down. Then in the confusion around the scaffolding, Root dodged out of sight, and a dummy was dangled high and riddled with real bullets.

During these early years of rodeo's development, William Frederick Cody continued to win fame and earn fortunes with his wild west troupe. His programs did not use the word "rodeo," but he selected the best riders and ropers to introduce this new sport of the American West to millions of people across the country.

In the 1890's, Buffalo Bill was at the zenith of his popularity. His Nebraska friends wanted to run him for governor; other admirers backed him for President of the United

States. When Chicago's Columbian Exposition, the World's Fair of 1893, barred the Wild West Show from its grounds because it was "too undignified," Cody rented fourteen acres opposite the fair grounds, set up a grandstand for 18,000 people, and started selling tickets. Every day thousands were turned away for lack of seats, and many a visitor paid his way into the Wild West Show, believing it to be the World's Fair.

Sir Henry Irving attended both, decided Buffalo Bill had the better show: "Such dare-devil riding was never seen on earth. When the American cowboys sweep like a tornado up the track, forty or fifty strong, every man swinging his hat and every pony at its utmost speed, a roar of wonder and delight breaks from the thousands in the grandstand."

It was inevitable that professional wild west show performers and rodeo contestants sometime would join forces for a grand extravaganza, and this event occurred at Cheyenne's second Frontier Days, September 1898. "Buffalo Bill's big outfit added over six hundred to the crowd," reported the Cheyenne *Daily Sun-Leader* of September 6. "Never in the previous history of the town have the streets presented so animated an appearance as they did this morning with crowds of cowboys, Indians of the Sioux, Arapahoe and Shoshone, and thousands of well-dressed people."

As the popularity of rodeo spread across the West and more and more cities began organizing annual shows, a few outstanding performers soon became famous. No official records were kept in the early days of the sport, but westerners seemed to know who the "champions" were.

Clay McGonigal of Texas was the "World's Champion Roper." He was beaten only once, and that time by Ellison Carroll, the first champion. Like Buffalo Bill's sharp-shooting Annie Oakley, Clay McGonigal's name became a noun in the terminology of wild west shows and rodeos. To all pioneer rodeo performers, a fast-roping exhibition was a "McGonigal."

Another early champion was Bill Pickett, the first bulldogger. According to rodeo legend, Pickett's method of downing steers originated the term "bulldogging." His technique has been graphically described by Colonel Zack Miller of the 101 Ranch: "He slid off a horse, hooked a steer with both hands on the horns, twisted its neck and then sunk his teeth into the steer's nostrils to bring him down."

After a tour of rodeos, Bill Pickett joined up with Miller Brothers 101 Ranch Show and became a first-rank star. He was one of the few great Negro rodeo performers. After he was killed in 1932 while roping a bronc, the Cherokee Strip Cowboy Association honored him by erecting a special marker at his grave, and Zack Miller wrote a poem to his memory.

Texas-born Leonard Stroud was the first All-Around Cowboy Champion. He was a bronc rider, a superb roper and bulldogger, and he introduced trick riding to many rodeos. Trick riders still perform his "Stroud Layout," in which the rider swings his body free from the horse with only one foot in stirrup, the other balanced against the saddle horn.

Among the early cowgirls in rodeo were Prairie Rose Henderson and Prairie Lillie

Allen. Prairie Rose started her career at Cheyenne as a bronc rider, and attracted so much attention that other rodeos soon introduced cowgirl bronc-busting contests as regular events. She decided rodeo costumes were too drab, and instead of the usual long divided skirt, Prairie Rose wore a short one of velvet with a brilliantly decorated hem. Her chief rival for the crown of champion cowgirl bronc rider was Prairie Lillie Allen. Prairie Lillie also did stunt riding for some of the early western moving pictures, and starred in circuses.

Lucille Mulhall was described as "the greatest cowgirl on earth" by Buffalo Bill Cody when he saw her perform. She could rope eight horses with one throw of the lariat. When President Theodore Roosevelt, an irrepressible cowboy himself, visited the Mulhall ranch, Lucille amazed him by roping a coyote from horseback.

The story of Lucille Mulhall's career has all the ingredients of a classic American tragedy. She became a public figure in 1904 with her appearances at the Louisiana Purchase Exposition in St. Louis. Her father, Colonel Zack Mulhall, brought together a lusty troupe of riders for this show; one of his stunts was to have a mounted rider board a ferris wheel. He also advertised a bullfight and sold eight thousand tickets, but the law interfered just before the fight was to begin. The disappointed customers expressed their feelings by setting fire to the canvas-draped arena.

After leaving her father's colorful aggregation, Lucille Mulhall worked with Tom Mix and Will Rogers in rodeo, performing in the first shows at Madison Square Garden. Later she was a queen of the silent western movies. She made a fortune and lost it. After riding wild horses for years without an accident, she died in an automobile crash. Her old friend, Foghorn Clancy, has written a poignant description of her funeral: "The day after Christmas she was buried on the last pitiful acres of the once great Mulhall ranch, as a wild and driving rain turned the ground into a quagmire and the horses strained to pull the hearse across the field."

Lucille Mulhall's fellow Oklahomans, Tom Mix and Will Rogers, used their skills to achieve national fame as stage and screen actors; their names are already a part of the legend of the American West. Tom Mix was a cowboy on the 101 Ranch and did his first rodeo work with Miller Brothers Wild West Show. Will Rogers also left off punching cattle to join a small wild west show under the name of the Cherokee Kid. In 1905, they reached New York's Madison Square Garden. A few years later, gum-chewing, rope-twirling Will Rogers was the star of the Ziegfeld Follies, while Tom Mix was Hollywood's king of the silent western movies.

Another southwesterner whose name has become almost a synonym for rodeo is Foghorn Clancy. Originally christened Frederick Melton Clancy, he lost his first two names while he was a newsboy on the streets of Mineral Wells, Texas. Because his voice sounded "like a foghorn at sea," he became Foghorn Clancy. It is doubtful if any of the thousands of rodeo performers and spectators who knew Foghorn during his half-century career as rodeo announcer, promoter, and handicapper, ever suspected that he had any other name.

Foghorn Clancy entered his first roping and riding contest at San Angelo, Texas, in 1898, and was promptly bucked off a bronco. He had scarcely picked himself up out of the dust when he was offered a job calling the succeeding events; the contest manager suspected that Foghorn's voice might be more spectacular than his bronc-busting abilities. The manager was right, and on that summer day in San Angelo, Foghorn Clancy began his long career which carried him to almost every rodeo, roundup and stampede in North America.

While rodeo was developing these pioneer heroes and heroines, the old wild west shows were beginning a slow decline. After his great success of the 1890's, Buffalo Bill had fallen on evil days; his health was failing, his family life was breaking apart; his numerous investments used up money faster than he could earn it. One by one his partners deserted him to start shows of their own—"Bill" shows they were called because they all copied the original. Hundreds of tawdry imitations of his exciting program format toured the country, disillusioning the customers.

Gordon William Lillie, Pawnee Bill, had the only wild west show that rivaled Cody's. After growing up in Oklahoma among the Pawnees, Gordon Lillie had taken a troupe of these Indians into the original Wild West Show of 1883. In later years he split with Cody and formed his own organization—Pawnee Bill's Far East. In 1908, Pawnee Bill rescued Buffalo Bill from bankruptcy, and the new organization became Buffalo Bill's Wild West and Pawnee Bill's Great Far East Combined.

But even the joint efforts of the two Bill's could not save the Wild West Show. Time had passed it by. After two farewell cross-country tours, with the aging Cody appearing in a carriage instead of on horseback, the public stopped buying tickets. A mortgage kept the show going for a few months, but it lost money through one hundred successive performances. Ironically, the Wild West Show made its last stand in Colorado, the heart of the land from which its name had come. There the sheriff's men moved in to foreclose. "The show business," said Cody, "isn't what it used to be." He retired to his Wyoming ranch. And Pawnee Bill went home to Oklahoma to promote rodeo shows.

As the wild west shows folded their tents forever, rodeo sprang to full growth. Veterans of the big tents moved into the rodeo arenas as pioneers of developing circuits that swung from Texas to California, from Cheyenne to Calgary, from Pendleton to Madison Square Garden.

The Pendleton Roundup was born in 1908, the year that Pawnee Bill temporarily rescued Buffalo Bill's show from financial disaster. Pendleton's baseball club that summer was as bankrupt as Buffalo Bill, and to help the team finish out the season, a group of Oregon cowboys staged a small rodeo in the ball park. They received five dollars each for their efforts—and stole the show from the ball-and-bat boys.

Two years later Pendleton Roundup had become big-time rodeo. As an added feature to the usual program, more than a thousand northwestern Indians set up their tipis on the grounds, donned their tribal costumes, and paraded on gaily bedecked ponies —making the Roundup one of the most dazzling rodeos in the West.

The golden boys of the early Pendleton competitions were Yakima Canutt and Art Acord. Both were champion riders for a while, but like a number of other outstanding rodeo competitors soon found themselves performing before the cranking movie cameras of southern California.

Last of the big rodeos to be organized was the Calgary Stampede. Canada's Alberta Province was the last stamping ground of frontier ranching in North America, and amateur roping and riding contests were held in Calgary in 1893. Some years afterwards, Tom Mix and Guy Weadick attempted to stage a full-fledged rodeo there, but the first Stampede was not held until 1912. Four Canadian ranchers backed the show, providing the largest money prizes ever before offered rodeo contests.

"The finest gathering of riders and ropers ever got together," reported the Calgary *Herald*. The Governor-General of Canada came to see the show and partook of a "typical roundup breakfast, prepared and served by men who had been in the country ever since the days of the open range." Bertha Blancett, Lucille Mulhall, and many other rodeo stars from the United States participated in the first Calgary Stampede.

And so, in the early years of the 20th century, the old wild west shows vanished and rodeo came to maturity. Modern rodeo has all the individual spirit of the western settlers, yet is as stylized as a bullfight or a ballet. The programs follow a classical pattern—grand entry, bronc riding, bulldogging, calf roping, steer riding, steer roping.

The wild west shows were based on riding and roping; the pageantry of modern rodeo in turn is borrowed from the wild west shows. The grand entry which opens every rodeo is pure Buffalo Bill with its swirl of brilliant costumes and pennants, patriotic music, swift-paced flashing hoofs, hats swept off, and trained ponies bowing to the crowds.

No two bronc riders and no two bucking mounts are alike, yet in a rodeo contest rigid rules must be followed. The rider can use only a plain halter, one rein, and a regulation saddle. He must stay aboard for ten seconds after he and his bronc spring from the chute. During those ten seconds he can be disqualified for changing hands on the rein, pulling leather, blowing a stirrup, or failing to keep his spur active. Both mount and rider are judged by a point system.

Bulldogging or steer wrestling is a timed event, a series of rapid actions beginning with the dogger leaping from his horse to grasp the steer by the horns. By twisting the horns, he forces the steer down until it lies flat upon the ground. No longer does he bite the steer's nose or lip as did Bill Pickett; instead modern rules protect the animal. For instance, if a dogger lands too far forward and drops the steer's head to the ground in a somersault, the animal must be allowed to gain its footing again before the throw is made.

Steer riding is much like bareback bronc riding. The rider has only a single rope for security and can use only one hand. To qualify, he must stay clear of the ground for eight to ten seconds. Judging is by a point system.

Rodeo rules require that calves be thrown by hand, with three of their feet tied together at the finish. Steers are roped by their heads and should be brought to a halt facing the roper's horse.

Trick riding came to rodeo by way of a troupe of Cossack daredevils imported by the 101 Ranch. Intrigued by the Cossacks' stunts on their galloping horses, western cowboys soon introduced variations to American rodeo. Colorful costumes seem to be a necessary part of trick riding, and it is quite possible that the outlandish western garb which in recent years has invaded rodeo arenas can be blamed directly on Cossacks and trick riders.

And every rodeo must have its clown, usually the "rube" type who rides a burro when he first appears in the arena. A direct descendant of combined circuses and wild west shows of the last century, the rodeo clown is in continual hot water throughout the events. Jake Hartman, the famous Sioux Indian clown of pioneer rodeo, commented recently: "A clown had to be a comic in the old days. Now the bulls have taken over. Now a clown needs to be a clever bullfighter. If a clown gets hooked in the pants the people think it funny. It's like the olden times when the gladiators fought hungry lions in the Roman arenas. The more risk to life and limb the more laughs from the populace."

BUFFALO BILL: RIDING AND ROPING WAS THE HEART OF HIS SHOW

For a quarter century, Buffalo Bill's Wild West and its many imitators based their performances primarily upon the riding and roping skills of western horsemen. A born showman, Cody was also a skilled rider and marksman himself.

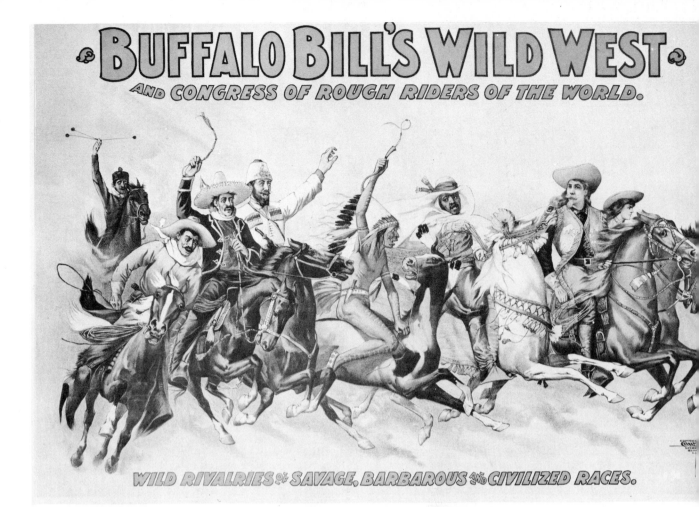

BUFFALO BILL'S WILD WEST AND CONGRESS OF ROUGH RIDERS OF THE WORLD.

WILD RIVALRIES of SAVAGE, BARBAROUS and CIVILIZED RACES.

THE WILD WEST SHOW: RODEO'S PROVING GROUND

In their search for amusement, western settlers developed rodeo, an original sport as American as baseball. Rodeo began in the roundup camps of cowboys, but before becoming an organized sport it was nurtured in the old wild west shows. The first modern rodeo may have been the rehearsals held at North Platte, Nebraska, in 1883, by Buffalo Bill Cody to select "cowboys, Mexican vaqueros, famous riders, and expert lasso throwers" for his wild west show.

COWBOYS RACING (on facing page, top)

It is no accident that the Spanish word for roundup, *rodeo*, came into use early as the American name for the most popular sport of the west. Rodeo was born out of competition among cowboys when they came together at roundup times. Rope-throwing contests and horse races were the usual activities at these spontaneous rodeos.

PECOS COWBOYS RELAXING (on facing page, bottom)

During the same summer that Buffalo Bill's Wild West took to the road, the first recorded roping and riding tournament was held in Texas. A few days before July 4, 1883, some cowboys got into a friendly argument in a Pecos City saloon (such as is shown here) over which outfit had the best bronc riders and steer ropers. They held a contest on Independence Day, using the courthouse yard as corral and the Pecos main street as arena.

THE UBIQUITOUS DEADWOOD STAGE

No wild west show was complete without its Deadwood Stage *(above)*, an act which was borrowed later by rodeos and is still occasionally used as a special feature.

PERFORMING FOR TENT SHOW AUDIENCE *(on facing page, top)*

But for many years local rodeo contests were purely amateur, and if an expert rider wanted to earn money with his skills he had to join a wild west show.

SOME FANCY ACTING *(on facing page, bottom)*

Bronc riders with the traveling tent shows dismounted occasionally to act in spectacular pageants such as this spirited (but unhistorical) defense of a Union Pacific Railroad train by woolly-chapped cowboys.

INDIANS

Indians, being natural riders, provided both color and an element of menace for the big acts in traveling shows. Later they were among the main attractions of outstanding rodeos such as the Pendleton Roundup.

VAQUEROS FROM MEXICO

Mexican vaqueros were also star performers. Mexican cowboys had staged roping and riding tournaments below the Rio Grande even before there was a cattle industry in the United States. One of their favorite stunts was throwing bulls by the tails.

PRESCOTT'S FRONTIER DAYS

Arizona Frontier Days at Prescott lays claim to being the "first organized rodeo," dating from July 4, 1888. The big prize that day went to a cowboy named Juan Leivas, who received the silver trophy shown *right*.

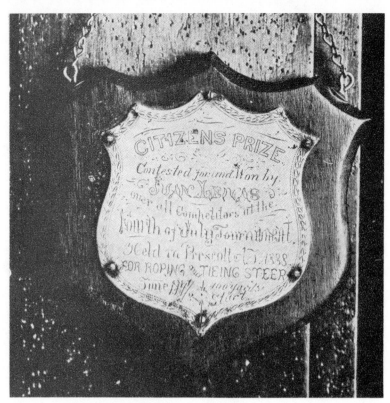

J. ELLISON CARROLL: FIRST CHAMPION ROPER

As there were no standard rules for rodeo contests, individual champions were not officially recognized in the early days of the sport. The first claimant to a championship was J. Ellison Carroll, who won a steer roping contest at Canadian, Texas, in 1888, and for the next quarter century beat out all his competitors.

BUCKAROOS OF THE NORTHWEST

Northwestern ropers and riders kept their contests on an amateur basis until 1893. Three pioneer professionals were Lee Caldwell, Jackson Sundown, and Yakima Canutt, *above*, left to right. Jackson Sundown, wearing the woolly chaps, was a nephew of the heroic Nez Percé, Chief Joseph. He won a riding championship at Pendleton when he was fifty years old and was billed as "the greatest rider of the red race."

BILL CODY'S COWBOYS

Meanwhile, William Frederick Cody was earning a fortune with his Wild West troupe. His programs did not use the word "rodeo," but his riders and ropers *(above)* were introducing this new sport of the American west to millions of people across the country. Cody selected the best cowboys the West could offer for his shows.

TROUPING IN THE "WILD WEST"

Westerners were Buffalo Bill's most loyal customers, and Cody loved trouping in the country where he had begun his colorful career. In 1898, he took his show to Cheyenne for the second Frontier Days celebration. "Buffalo Bill's big outfit added over six hundred to the crowd," reported the Cheyenne *Daily Sun-Leader,* September 6. "Never in the previous history of the town have the streets presented so animated an appearance as they did this morning with crowds of cowboys, Indians of the Sioux, Arapahoe and Shoshone, and thousands of well-dressed people."

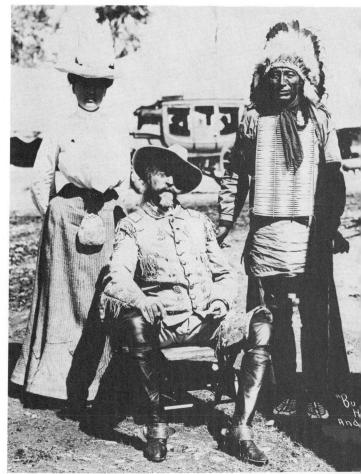

THE COWBOY BAND, CHICAGO, 1893

When Cody arrived in Chicago in 1893 to play the great Columbian Exposition, his Wild West Show was barred from the grounds because it was "too undignified." He rented fourteen acres opposite the fair, set up a grandstand for 18,000 people, and started selling tickets. It was a daily sellout; many a visitor paid his way into the Wild West Show, believing it to be the Exposition. The cowboy band of 1893 *(illustrated)* was a feature soon to be adopted by many rodeos.

ACTION AT CHEYENNE

Cheyenne's Frontier Days was the first big-time rodeo, a commercial venture supported by local businessmen and the Union Pacific Railroad. This photograph of Leonard Stroud on Indian Tom at Cheyenne, is an early action picture which in its time was considered the most notable rodeo photograph ever made.

WILL ROGERS, RODEO ROPER

In 1905, a western rodeo troupe traveled to New York to exhibit its skills in Madison Square Garden. One of the ropers was the Cherokee Kid, a former Oklahoma cow-puncher who had been working with a small wild west show. The Cherokee Kid's real name was Will Rogers, and within a short time this gum-chewing rope twirler was star of the Ziegfeld Follies and on his way to national fame. He is shown between George W. Saunders and Ab Blocker, veteran trail drivers.

TOM MIX

Tom Mix, another Oklahoman, was also a member of the first Madison Square Garden rodeo troupe, and, like Will Rogers, he went on to achieve renown as Hollywood's king of the silent western movies. Shown with Tom Mix in the photograph *above* are bronco rider Leonard Stroud on *left*, and rodeo photographer R. R. Doubleday on *right*.

THE "STROUD LAYOUT" (on facing page, top)

In the early days of rodeo no official records were kept, but westerners seemed to know who the "champions" were. Texas-born Leonard Stroud was known as the first All-Around-Cowboy champion, but his specialty was trick riding. Rodeo contestants are still performing his "Stroud Layout," in which the body is swung free from the horse with only one foot in stirrup, the other balanced against the saddle horn.

BILL PICKETT (on facing page, bottom)

Another early champion was Bill Pickett *(left)* who originated bulldogging. His technique has been graphically described by Colonel Zack Miller of the 101 Ranch: "He slid off a horse, hooked a steer with both hands on the horns, twisted its neck and then sunk his teeth in the steer's nostrils to bring him down."

DEL BLANCETT

Here Del Blancett shows how old-time bulldoggers finished their stunts by biting the steer's lip and holding their hands free. Nostril and lip biting were banned from rodeos in later years.

TILLIE BALDWIN

Western women entered rodeo competition in 1897, one of the pioneers being Tillie Baldwin. Billed as "the only woman bulldogger in the world," Tillie also introduced the "Roman Stand" and for several years was champion cowgirl trick rider.

LUCILLE MULHALL ROPING FOUR

"The greatest cowgirl on earth," said Buffalo Bill Cody when he saw Lucille Mulhall perform. She could rope from four to eight horses with one throw of the lariat. When President Theodore Roosevelt, an irrepressible rodeo fan, visited the Mulhall ranch, Lucille amazed him by roping a coyote from horseback.

BERTHA BLANCETT WINNING LADIES' ROMAN RACE

Bertha Blancett was "champion lady bronco buster of the world." In the winters, when rodeos were inactive, she worked in Hollywood as a stunt rider for the old Bison Moving Picture Company. She could down a galloping horse with the suddenness of a pistol shot. Here she is shown winning the Ladies' Roman Race at Pendleton Roundup.

SOME OF THE "BILL" SHOWMEN

As rodeo increased in popularity, the wild west shows began a slow decline. One by one Buffalo Bill's partners left him to start shows of their own—"Bill shows" they were called because they all imitated the original. *Above* are some "Bill" showmen whose organizations were better than the usual: left to right *(standing)* Deadwood Dick, Dr. W. F. Carver, Idaho Bill; *(seated)* Luther North, Pawnee Bill, Diamond Dick.

PAWNEE BILL AND MAE LILLIE *(on facing page, top)*

Gordon William Lillie, Pawnee Bill had the only wild west show that rivaled Cody's. After growing up in Oklahoma among the Pawnees, Gordon Lillie had taken a troupe of these Indians into the original Wild West Show of 1883. In later years he split with Cody and formed his own organization. His wife, Mae Lillie, was the "little sure-shot" of Pawnee Bill's Far East—as he called his show. In 1908, Pawnee Bill rescued Cody from bankruptcy, and the new organization became Buffalo Bill's Wild West and Pawnee Bill's Great Far East Combined.

PAWNEE BILL AT PRINCETON *(on facing page, bottom)*

Always an intrepid showman, Pawnee Bill took his performers into places where others never would have dared to go. This photograph shows the beginning of a street brawl between Pawnee Bill's parading horsemen and students of Princeton University, 1899.

TEX COOPER

Miller Brothers 101 Ranch was the last of the great wild west shows, but even with such popular stars as Tex Cooper (*left*) this traveling ranch rodeo soon went into bankruptcy.

BUFFALO BILL'S FAREWELL

Even the joint efforts of Pawnee Bill and Buffalo Bill could not save the Wild West Show. Time had passed it by. After two farewell cross-country tours, with the aging Cody appearing in a carriage instead of on horseback, the public stopped buying tickets. Ironically, the Wild West Show made its last stand in Colorado, the heart of the land from which its name had come. There the sheriff's men moved in to foreclose. "The show business," said Cody, "isn't what it used to be."

RODEO AT THE GRASS ROOTS

Rodeo in the meantime was becoming more and more popular among westerners. When farmers and ranchers drove their buggies and early model autos to their local county fairs (such as this one at Broken Bow, Nebraska), they expected to see or participate in roping and riding contests. An Iowan recalling his boyhood has told of attending a county fair where two cowboys "dressed up in leather britches, red flannel shirts and broad brimmed hats rode into the ring and took after a little herd of wild horses. After a good deal of galloping and circling around, they roped one of them and threw him down so hard we thought it surely had broken his neck."

GRAND ENTRY

In the first decade of the 20th century, rodeo reached its maturity, adopting some of the pageantry of knighthood, some of the roping and riding of roundup camps, some of the circus of wild west shows. The grand entry *(above)* which opens every rodeo is pure Buffalo Bill with its swirl of colorful costumes and pennants, its patriotic music, swift-paced ponies, and hats swept off in flourishes to the cheering crowds.

The Round UP Clown" Pendleton Ore Moorhouse

RODEO CLOWN

Derived from the wild west shows and tent circuses is the rodeo clown. Every rodeo has one, usually a "rube" type who rides a burro. "A clown had to be a comic in the old days," Jake Herman, the famous Sioux Indian clown of pioneer rodeo, said recently. "Now the bulls have taken over. Now a clown needs to be a clever bullfighter. If a clown gets hooked in the pants the people think it funny. It's like the olden times when the gladiators fought hungry lions in the Roman arenas. The more risk to life and limb the more laughs from the populace."

YAKIMA CANUTT

As rodeo became a standardized sport, it developed its own stars who were as well known as the champions of other sports. The golden boy of Pendleton's early years was Yakima Canutt *(right)*, who later went to Hollywood to perform before cranking movie cameras in epics of the western range.

Yakima Canutt

EAGLES HELPING ART ACORD UP
AFTER WINNING THE CHAMPIONSHIP

PITCHIN' HIGH AND PITCHIN' STRAIGHT

And in the rodeo arena the horse remains the king. No printed regulations forbid a horse to sidewind, corkscrew, skyscrape, sunfish, or high dive; and all the cowboy and rodeo associations in the world can't keep a rider in the saddle for ten seconds if the horse decides otherwise.

ART ACORD (on facing page, top)

Art Acord was another buckaroo and bulldogger who won fame as a rodeo champion before he became the hero of millions of western fans in the silent movie era. (Man on left is standing by to assist Art Acord in getting clear of steer after the animal has been bulldogged.)

SPINNING A CRITTER (on facing page, bottom)

With the passing of the years, rodeo has become more and more professional, bound by numerous associations and regulations. But the sport remains the favored one of the West. The odds are still on the calf or steer every time a roper takes off across the arena swinging his loop. The spectators still come up cheering when the lariat snaps tight and the critter goes spinning into the dust.

CHAPTER EIGHT

LAW, ORDER
AND POLITICS

FORMS AND CEREMONIES are at a discount, and generosity has its home in the pure air of the Rocky Mountains," wrote Thomas Dimsdale, Oxford graduate, singing-school teacher, and editor of the *Montana Post* in 1865. Another Briton, a cowboy named John J. Fox, observed in Wyoming that "democracy was practiced at its best and purest form at this time and place."

Dimsdale and Fox were idealists and probably over-simplified the state of law and order in the old West. Informal, direct, and democratic, the first westerners truly were; but they also had an instinct for group organization that began with the Lewis and Clark expedition, developed into complex printed constitutions for the government of overland parties crossing the plains in the gold rush of 1849, and became full blown in the elaborate secret rituals of the Grange and its political successors of the late 19th century.

Before he reached his destination, almost every emigrant to the west recognized the power of law in the person of his wagon master or the commander of his overland company:

"The commander shall have entire and complete control. . . .

"There shall be no exemption from any service. . . .

"We do solemnly and mutually pledge to each other, our lives, our fortunes, and our sacred honors."

But the first western settlements, being under loose territorial control, had neither laws nor officers for enforcement. Petty thieving and crimes of violence were generally unknown in the homesteading country, but the mining settlements and cattle-shipping towns often became so lawless that the only cure was "a short cord and a good drop." When conditions became unbearable, the more respectable citizens would call a meeting

216

to select a Justice of the Peace. Justices more often than not were elected by voice vote, as was Richard C. Barry of Sonora, a former Texas ranger turned California gold miner.

One of Dick Barry's decisions:

"N. B. Barber, the lawyer for George Work, insolently told me there were no law for me to rool so. I told him that I didn't care a damn for his book law, that I was the law myself. I fined him $50 and committed him to gaol 5 days for contempt of court in bringing my roolings and dississions into disreputableness and as a warning to unrooly persons not to contradict this court."

Violence fed on violence in the booming polyglot communities of the West—in Onion Valley, Panamint, Tailholt, Skidoo, in Tucson, Dodge City, Rawhide, Abilene, Brewery Gulch, and Bannock. Every mining town had its "hang tree," and every trail town had its "boot hill." Many an outlaw received a "suspended sentence" from the famed old hang tree in Helena's Dry Gulch. In San Francisco, the vigilantes hanged their victims from a wharf derrick on Market Street. In Tombstone, they were left dangling from convenient telegraph poles.

Bad men and good men had no more use for the old-fashioned *code duello* than they had for a formal gallows. "Calling a man a liar, a thief, or a son-of-a-bitch was provocation sufficient to justify instant slaying."

In San Francisco, a group of desperadoes did some organizing on their own, committing robberies, rapes, murders and arson. Late at night they roamed the streets in bands, barking like dogs at the respectable citizenry, who named them the Hounds. Courts could do nothing with them; as a New England visitor observed, the jurors were as bad as the Hounds, chatting and winking and smirking at the judge, and smoking with the accused.

But by 1861, the West was sufficiently organized to take sides on the issues of the onrushing Civil War. One strong faction wanted to go with the South; another proposed a separate Republic of the Pacific. The far West, with California in the van, seemed to be moving toward separation from the Union.

On May 11, however, along San Francisco's Market Street—where only a few years earlier vigilantes were hanging men to keep the peace—a group of Union supporters rallied around the bannered words of Daniel Webster: "The Union, the whole Union, and nothing but the Union."

Before the day ended, almost everybody in San Francisco gathered in the muddy street to join the tumultuous meeting. Men came on foot, on horseback, in carriages; the crowd blocked the horse-drawn street cars, swarmed over water carts and bread wagons, climbed upon roofs and packing boxes and barrels so that they could see the speakers' stand.

A few days later, California's legislature voted to support the Union, and all the West followed its example. Law, order, and politics were now well-established beyond the Mississippi River.

During the wild years when society in the West was without "forms and ceremonies," the women who had crossed the plains and mountains gradually discovered that they were a free sex. At first, only a few realized that law, order and politics no longer barred them from doing as they pleased. But the others caught on fairly rapidly. "They were treated with a deference and liberality unknown in other climes," commented the observant Thomas Dimsdale in what soon proved to be an understatement. Western women busted loose from centuries of law and order and started a revolution which is still spreading around the world.

Throughout the period of western settlement, men outnumbered women two to one —in some places thirty to one. But then as now, mere numerical superiority was of no consequence in the war between the sexes.

Britisher John J. Fox noted signs of the revolution in 1885 when he arrived in Carbon, Wyoming, to begin his ranching career. As Fox walked up into the town from the railroad depot, he met a cowboy and a girl "dashing down the street on horses, yelling, the man firing several shots in the air. He was evidently well 'lit up,' and the noisy female rode astride her pony, her long hair streaming behind her. She had on nothing but a chemise. To a very green young man raised in the most conservative little country town in Wessex, this was Life with a capital L. How my eminently respectable Victorian training leapt to meet it!"

A correspondent for the Missouri *Statesman*, visiting the California gold mines, wrote his newspaper that he had seen a woman in a gambling house, "sitting quietly at the monte table, dressed in white pants, blue coat, and cloth cap, curls dangling over her cheeks, cigar in her mouth and a glass of punch at her side. She handled a pile of doubloons with her blue-kid-gloved hands and bet most boldly."

And California women were way ahead of the bloomer craze in the East, according to a San Francisco newspaper of 1851: "The city was taken quite by surprise yesterday afternoon by observing a woman in company with her male companion, crossing the lower side of the Plaza. She was magnificently arrayed in a black satin skirt, very short, with flowing red satin trousers, a splendid yellow crape shawl and a silk turban *a la Turque*. She really looked magnificent and was followed by a large retinue of men and boys, who appeared to be highly pleased with the style."

In Wyoming Territory, December 10, 1869, for the first time on this continent, women were invested with "all the political rights, duties, franchises, and responsibilities of male citizens." A dozen years later, the editor of the *Laramie Weekly Sentinel* was still trying to figure out how it happened. "The motives which prompted the legislature to lay aside its conservatism and take this new departure were, so far as can be judged, an ambition to immortalize themselves and out-Herod Herod." On second thought, he suspected the legislature may have been "influenced by the idea that this act would materially serve to advertise our young territory and bring it into notoriety abroad."

Whatever the reason for this remarkable action on the part of the Wyoming lawmakers in giving women the vote, both major political parties began vying with each other for support from the new voters, providing fine horse carriages to transport them to the polls.

Margaret Thomson Hunter has told of how she voted the first year Wyoming became a state: "When election day rolled around, Mr. Hellman stopped in and asked me to go and vote for him. I was busy making pies and hadn't intended voting, but after all Mr. Hellman was a neighbor and also a very good friend of my husband's. So I pushed my pies aside, removed my apron, and tidied myself up a bit. Then I got into the buggy with Mr. Hellman and he drove me to the polls. Well, I voted and as we turned to leave we came face to face with my husband. When I explained to him that I had just voted for Mr. Hellman, I thought he would have a fit.

"You see, my husband was a staunch Democrat and one of the leaders in his party, and there I had just voted for a Republican. He was never so humiliated in all his life, he told me."

Running for office was a strenuous task in the geographically enormous western counties and states. Voters were scattered over vast distances, and roads and trails were often impassable. During one campaign, a Wyoming candidate traveled fifteen hundred miles by buckboard, attending forty-five political rallies—which in Wyoming always ended with dancing well past midnight. Because of their new political power, he felt compelled to dance with every woman present.

In spite of all this, there were candidates a-plenty for every office. According to the editor of the Leavenworth (Kansas) *Weekly Herald,* there were often more candidates than voters: "Dr. H————— tells a good story at the expense of our worthy ex-city marshal. While the latter was endeavoring to rescue the team which broke through the ice on election day, he broke through himself, and came very near drowning. As the ice was giving way, and he about going down, he exclaimed at the top of his voice: 'I have not voted—I have not voted!' Of course he was rescued, as candidates could be found within hearing of every man's voice."

Western politicians wanted everybody to vote, on occasion even welcomed the poor and voteless Indians. "Yuma was a hell of a place when I first went there in 1870," said Frederic G. Brecht, an old settler of Prescott, Arizona. "The politicians would bring a string of Yuma Indians up to vote. They wore nothing but a breech-cloth and perhaps a stovepipe hat, and held their already marked tickets in their hand. When a clerk would ask an Indian his name he would say 'Sullivan' or 'Malony,' or any other good Irish name he had been drilled in saying."

After the Panic of 1873 and the years immediately following, the westerners' capacity for ready organization was demonstrated when they rushed by thousands to form local and state units of the Patrons of Husbandry, or National Grange. The Grange had been started in the East by Oliver Hudson Kelley in 1867, but met with small success until the outraged western farmers suddenly put all their reckless vigor into it. Settlers beyond the Mississippi were angry over the high prices they had to pay for things they had to buy and the low prices they received for things they had to sell. They were not only disgusted with grasshoppers and drouths, they were fighting mad against the railroad monopoly which raised rates higher and higher until there was no profit in shipping products to eastern markets.

"Let the public be damned," said Commodore Cornelius Vanderbilt, spokesman for the railroads, and the westerners began buzzing like angry bees. They welcomed the National Grange with its secret rituals and hopeful expectations. Across the dusty plains of Kansas and Nebraska, and far out into Colorado, Montana, and Washington, long processions of buggies were rolling to Grange meetings. In front were the banners and crudely lettered mottoes of the lodges, with sometimes a band playing, and marshals on horseback in red sashes galloping up and down the columns, keeping them moving in orderly fashion.

To eliminate middlemen and keep prices low for the things they had to buy, the Grangers entered into an agreement with a young Chicago drummer who had been traveling through rural areas selling bargain merchandise to farmers. The traveling salesman's name was Montgomery Ward, and in 1872 he issued a single-sheet catalog for members of the Grange. Three years later his catalog had seventy-two pages with illustrations—one of them featuring a "Grange hat."

Montgomery Ward's catalog was particularly welcomed by Granger wives, who being western women had of course become members of the new organization along with their men. Caroline Arabella Hall of Minnesota, niece of the founder, had taken care of this by traveling all the way to Washington to insist on women being admitted. Caroline Hall won her suit against much opposition from some male members who thought that admitting women to equal membership in a secret society was "going altogether too far."

No longer could the western settler leave his wife in a lonely farmhouse while he rode off to town on horseback for an evening of revelry with his lodge brothers. Now he had to hitch a team to the buggy and ride sedately to the schoolhouse, to listen to Grange debates and lectures, and sing songs out of a Grange song book compiled by Miss Caroline Arabella Hall.

By the late 1870's, many westerners lost their warm enthusiasm for the Grange movement. They thought its aims were admirable, but the railroads, the banks and the government paid no attention. And prices for everything the farmers bought kept going up; prices for everything the farmers sold kept going down.

About this time, far out in Lampasas County, Texas, a group of ranchers and farmers organized the Texas Alliance to combat cattle and horse thieves, barbed wire, and land-sharks. They had secret signs, grips, and passwords. Like the Grange, they also attempted to eliminate middlemen through cooperative buying and selling. Within a few years the Alliance spread across all of Texas, north into Kansas and Nebraska, and then moved westward.

Unlike the Grange, this new organization was keenly interested in politics and soon attracted thousands of non-farmers into its ranks—preachers, teachers, editors, and country doctors, persons whose livelihood depended upon the prosperity of farmers. "The Grange had been social," said Hamlin Garland, who was just beginning his literary career as a partisan journalist, "but the Farmers' Alliance came as a revolt."

An outstanding leader of the Alliance was Jerry Simpson, a mild-mannered Kansas farmer with a Scotch burr in his voice. Originally a Great Lakes sailor, Jerry Simpson had ventured to Kansas in the great wave of western land settlement. "I came to Kansas to plant something in the ground and see it grow and reproduce its kind," he said. Jerry Simpson also had a yen to be a politician, and he took for his motto: "I love my fellow man."

He changed from an Abraham Lincoln supporter to a Greenbacker; in succession he was a Granger, a Union Labor man, and a Single Taxer. He won his colorful nickname in his first campaign for Congress as an Alliance candidate running against a powerful Republican lawyer from Wichita. When the Republican press called Jerry Simpson a clown, an ignoramus, a boor, and a ragamuffin, he retaliated by describing his opponent as "Prince Hal, a prince of royal blood who travels in his special car, his dainty person gorgeously bedecked in silk stockings."

William Allen White, then a young reporter, immediately dubbed Simpson "the Sockless Socrates." Sockless Jerry Simpson he was from that time on, glorying in the portrait which his opponents made of him as an ignorant fool. Actually he was an avid reader of Dickens, Carlyle, Scott, Burns, the Bible, Tom Paine, and the *Congressional Record*.

"It was an era of fervent meetings and fulminating resolutions," said Hamlin Garland, who was traveling through the rebellious west in 1890 as correspondent for the *Arena*. "I attended barbecues on drab and dusty fairgrounds, meeting many of the best known leaders in the field." It was the day of the political picnic, the day of the orator with waving arms and flapping coattails, of eloquence so emotional that speaker and audience wept streams of tears.

And women were everywhere in this political revolt. "Farmers' wives and daughters rose earlier and worked later to gain time to cook the picnic dinners, to paint the mottoes on the banners, to practice with the glee clubs, to march in processions . . . in that wonderful picnicking, speech-making Alliance summer of 1890."

Eighteen-ninety was the year that Mary Elizabeth Lease, leading woman orator in the western revolt, made her most famous speech at a political picnic on the fairgrounds of Paola, Kansas: "The people are at bay. Let the bloodhounds of money who have dogged us thus far beware. What you farmers need is to *raise less corn and more hell!*"

Mary E. Lease became a legend in her own time. Born in Ireland of a nonconformist father who had fled to Pennsylvania, she had come to Kansas in the early 1870's to earn a living by teaching school. She married Charles Lease, and lived the lonely life of a farmer's wife until a mortgage forclosure forced them to move into Wichita where Lease could earn a little money as a pharmacist. Mary Elizabeth took in washing and read law until she was swept up into the Alliance movement.

Wearing her high-collared black dress, Mary Lease toured the farming country and made 161 speeches in the campaign of 1890. She was a long-legged, fair-skinned, dark-haired woman with a prominent chin and melancholy blue eyes. She hypnotized herself as well as her audiences with her golden contralto voice. "There were times when I actually made speeches without knowing it, when I was surprised to read in the morning paper that I had spoken the night before . . . My tongue is loose at both ends and hung on a swivel."

After hearing her for the first time, a western farmer recorded in his diary: "Went to town to hear Joint discussion between Mrs. Lease & John M. Brumbaugh. Poor Brumbaugh was not in it."

The dynamic Alliance drew into its ranks Grangers, Greenbackers, Singletaxers—all the voices of dissent in the West. "The campaign of 1890," commented the Kansas City *Times*, "was a good deal more than a political campaign . . . it was a religious revival, a crusade."

Alliance parades moved through the streets of villages and towns. Protesting farmers with their wives and children rode on hayrack floats, singing gospel tunes with new words. *The Kingdom of Mammon Shall Fall* was a favorite:

> "There's a grand reformation
> Have you heard the welcome tune?
> It is sweeping through our nation
> 'Tis a mighty power grown."

Torchlight parades were so popular that salesmen toured the plains country selling rubber capes to protect the marchers from sparks. Crudely lettered placards bobbed along the lines of march: WE ARE MORTGAGED, ALL BUT OUR VOTES. SPECIAL PRIVILEGE FOR NONE, EQUAL RIGHTS FOR ALL. DOWN WITH WALL STREET. And there was usually a float crowded with pretty girls knitting socks for Sockless Jerry Simpson.

And when the ballots were counted after the elections of 1890, the nation was startled by the power of the farmers' revolt. In Kansas alone, they elected a Senator, four Congressmen, and ninety-one state legislators. In Nebraska, their success was almost as great; in Colorado, the Dakotas, and Minnesota, they controlled the balance of power.

The victories of 1890 stimulated agitation for organization of a third political party in the United States. Throughout 1891 and into 1892, conventions were held in various cities, while thousands of unemployed miners in the far West were swelling the ranks of the rebellious.

At St. Louis in December 1891, delegates went wild when their leaders presented a Populist Manifesto calling for a national convention to nominate a presidential candidate for the new People's Party. "Everyone was upon his feet in an instant and thundering cheers from 10,000 throats greeted these demands as the road to liberty. Hats, papers, handkerchiefs, etc., were thrown into the air; wraps, umbrellas and parasols waved; cheer after cheer thundered and reverberated through the vast hall, reaching the outside of the building where thousands, who had been awaiting the outcome, joined in the applause till for blocks in every direction the exultation made the din indescribable. For fully ten minutes the cheering continued, reminding one of the lashing of the ocean against a rocky beach during a hurricane."

The hurricane lashed across the west to Omaha, where on July 4, 1892, the new People's Party nominated General James B. Weaver of Iowa to run for President against the candidates of the two old parties. Weaver lacked the color of Sockless Jerry Simpson and Mary E. Lease, but as a loyal follower described him, he was a composite of strength and gentleness: "The cannibalism of politics has snapped at him in vain."

The delegates gave Weaver an ovation but reserved their most enthusiastic applause for the reading of the new party's platform, a sacred creed designed to bring back prosperity to the settlers of the western land. After its reading, the band played *Yankee Doodle* for twenty minutes.

Among western leaders campaigning for the Populists in that dramatic political year of 1892 was Senator William Alfred Peffer of Kansas. "Formerly the man who lost his farm could go west," he said. "Now there is no longer any west to go to. Now they have to fight for their homes instead of making new." Even in a day when beards were common, the facial adornment of Senator Peffer was so lengthy it attracted national attention. Political cartoonists had a field day with Peffer's beard. One newspaper commented: "Senator Peffer is not obliged to spend money for a Christmas tree. He simply puts glass balls, small candles, strings of pop-corn and cornucopias in his magnificent whiskers and there you are."

In Colorado, Davis Waite launched into a campaign for governor on the Populist ticket, emphasizing the new party's platform proposal for "free and unlimited coinage of silver." Waite was a printer, editor and lawyer, a headstrong zealot, a master of rich rhetoric. "It is better, infinitely better," he cried, "that blood should flow to the horses' bridles rather than our national liberties should be destroyed."

Known thereafter as "Bloody Bridles" Waite, he terrified conservatives with his threats to coin state money for Colorado, to lead the silver states out of the Union—and if need be, invade the East with an armed body of Populist cavalry. "Mr. Waite comes from a fine New England family," said one of his friends, "but sometimes he has rather peculiar notions." In spite of his "peculiar notions," Waite rode to victory over his old-party opponents.

Another ardent Populist supporter was Hamlin Garland, who had grown to manhood on his father's prairie homestead and had seen the bright promises of the western horizon turn into poverty and endless toil. Rejecting it all, Garland had fled eastward to Boston where he hoped to earn a living by teaching and writing. Now he returned to his west to join the Populist crusade. He wrote a propaganda novel, *Prairie Folks,* joined the staff of a periodical supporting the cause, and offered his services as a campaign speaker.

"With other eager young reformers, I rode across the odorous prairie swells, journeying from one meeting place to another, feeling as my companions did that something grandly beneficial was about to be enacted into law. In this spirit I spoke at Populist picnics, standing beneath great oaks, surrounded by men and women, workworn like my own father and mother, shadowed by the same cloud of dismay. I smothered in small halls situated over saloons and livery stables, traveling by freight-train at night in order to ride in triumph as 'Orator of the Day' at some county fair, until at last I lost all sense of being the writer and recluse."

The noisy campaigning of the Populists was heard across the nation. Although most contemporary newspapers and periodicals were sympathetic toward the plight of western farmers, few were friendly toward the new third party which they believed to be a threat to the American political system. The presidential election of 1892 was an unorthodox affair, with voters crossing party lines in all directions. When it was all over, the Populists were victorious only in the West, while the rest of the country elected Grover Cleveland and a Democratic government.

In Kansas, the Populists had won their most spectacular victories, electing the governor and a large majority of state senators. They also claimed the state House of Representatives, but the Republicans disputed this. Leaders of the third party gathered in Topeka in January, 1893, to celebrate the inauguration of the "first People's Party administration on earth," but arguments over control of the House dampened the proceedings.

The Populists and the Republicans each elected a presiding officer for the House, and for several days each side took turns passing laws and making speeches. Finally the Republicans announced that after one more week they would bar from the floor all who refused to recognize their organization as the legally elected House. When the Republicans adjourned for the day, Populists armed with rifles took possession of the legislative halls. Next morning, the Republicans smashed in the doors with sledge hammers, and the Governor called out the state militia. "War times in Topeka," a Kansas farmer recorded in his journal; but the Gatling guns which rolled out upon the capitol grounds were harmless; some one had stolen all the cranks necessary to operate them.

A Kansas blizzard interrupted action for several hours, and when the weather cleared the Populists agreed to leave the dispute to the courts. As the courts were controlled by Republicans, this retreat of the Populists amounted to a surrender. From that day the People's Party was on the defensive in Kansas. Some months afterwards, the Concordia *Empire* slyly observed: "Pops don't spring up out of the bushes now by the thousands as they did three or four years ago."

But the money panic of 1893 brought more unrest across the west. Miners, loggers, and workers in the new cities were soon in a worse plight than the mortgaged farmers. Proposed remedies for the situation were as numerous as the unemployed, but the Free Silver advocates seemed to be winning the most followers.

On a summer day in 1893, a huge bearded man, wearing high boots, a sombrero, and a fringed buckskin shirt with buttons made of silver dollars, arrived in Chicago to attend a Free Silver convention. He was Carl Browne of San Francisco, rancher, cartoonist, editor, dreamer, emotional orator, and inventor of flying machines. His friends called him "Old Greasy" because he seldom took time to bathe.

During the convention, Browne made the acquaintance of mild-mannered Jacob Coxey of Ohio and convinced him that an army of a million westerners was ready to march on Washington to demand action from the government. Coxey thought that perhaps a million easterners might also join the march, and so he and Browne began the organization of Coxey's Army. Browne was responsible for the slogans, the badges, and other publicity for the Great March, "the petition in boots," as he called it.

Coxey's Army consisted of dozens of armies rather than one, and they all began moving toward Washington in the spring of 1894. Coordination of operations was completely lacking, however, with Browne and Coxey devoting all their energies to the comparatively short march from Massillon, Ohio. The largest armies were formed in the far West, in California, Washington, Colorado, Idaho, and Montana.

In Butte, a group of unemployed miners and railroad workers kicked up a storm by seizing a Northern Pacific freight train. They ran it to Bozeman, picked up some new recruits and three tons of flour and beef, and continued to Billings. Here they were met by a United States marshal and seventy-five deputies who demanded an unconditional surrender. In the fight which followed, one man was killed and several wounded; the marshal and his deputies beat a hasty retreat.

While the train rolled on to Forsyth to sidetrack for the night, War Department headquarters in Washington, D. C., was ordering six companies of infantry from Fort Keogh and four troops of cavalry from Fort Custer to march out and capture the stolen train. About midnight, while the Coxeyites were asleep in the box cars, their sentinels saw a train approaching from the east at high speed. Before the sleeping men could be awakened, the oncoming train stopped, and six companies of infantry swarmed out of it. The civilian "army" of 331 men surrendered; they were taken to Helena as prisoners, were tried, and given light sentences. One month later this determined division of Coxy's Army was headed east again, going down the Missouri River in flatboats.

The largest army from the West originated in California, its leader being Charles T. Kelly, a San Francisco printer, a small, soft-spoken man with light blue eyes. Kelly and his 1500 followers (among whom was Jack London, the writer) also commandeered trains. The railroads were willing to cooperate by providing a special freight train, but Kelly's men wanted passenger cars. "We are United States citizens, not hogs," said Kelly.

When the army bogged down in Utah for lack of transportation, "Bloody Bridles" Waite, the fiery Populist governor of Colorado, invited them into his state. But the Rio Grande Western Railroad refused to ride them for free. Finally, Kelly's men seized a Union Pacific freight train, which they manned and rode all the way to Omaha with no opposition from the railroad.

But by the time the western divisions of Coxey's Army reached Washington, they found the first arrivals hungry, disgruntled, and divided into factions. Coxey had already left the city to raise more funds; Carl Browne and sixty of his lieutenants had departed for Atlantic City to bathe in the ocean.

The westerners stuck it out longer than most of the others, but at last they also admitted the Great March was a failure. "We are going back to our homes," said one Californian, "where we will continue the fight for liberty and equality at the ballot box."

Meanwhile in Nebraska, 34-year-old William Jennings Bryan was laying plans to insure that his name would be on the next presidential ballot as the choice of the rebellious westerners. Bryan had just lost an election race for United States Senator to a Populist, and thereupon decided that what his Democratic Party needed was an infusion of new blood from the dynamic People's Party. Borrowing practically all of the Populists' 1892 platform, Bryan began his campaign to be nominated for President by the Democrats in 1896.

The Silver Knight, as he was soon to be called, was an odd sort of westerner. In his black cutaway coat, low-cut vest, string tie, and soft felt hat, he looked like a politician from the deep South. He disliked whiskey; as a small boy working the harvests, he refused to carry any alcohol to the threshing hands, insisted they drink water instead. His voice ("clear and silvery as a bell") might have been that of an imploring, Bible-Belt evangelist.

But the West's Democrats and the West's Populists backed him from the beginning in the Chicago convention. His "Nebraska boys" wore red bandannas, waving them like provocative flags at the opposition delegates. Bryan's "cross of gold" speech won him the nomination, and shortly afterwards the Populist candidate of 1892, General Weaver, gave the Silver Knight his party's blessing.

Bryan campaigned everywhere, day and night. He wore out his staff and the newspaper men assigned to report his tour of the nation. "Bryan's youth and strength," commented one of these reporters, "stand him in good stead for his continual jaunting through the country. An older man could not go through the ordeal and live."

It seemed that everyone wanted to see him. Old ladies in sunbonnets trotted along the tracks beside his train, fifes and drums marched ahead of him in the streets, bands played "See the Conquering Hero Comes," the shrieks of the crowds became delirium. He averaged thirty speeches a day. Millions of Americans heard and saw this wild tornado from the plains.

But, as the campaign progressed, it became evident that he was making enemies as well as friends. He was called a tool of the capitalist silver interests, an anarchist, a blasphemer, an anti-Christ, "a mouthing, slobbering demagogue." At least one attempt was made to poison him.

Bryan did not win the election, but he came very close. 20,000 votes more would have taken him into the White House. He missed carrying Kentucky by 281 votes, California by 962, Oregon by 1,000.

Twice again, Bryan was to make his try for the presidency. But the West, along with the rest of the country, was entering upon a period of prosperity and organized protests were no longer popular. There would be no more western political uprisings for another generation.

While western politicians were making history—if not winning elections—the appointed keepers of the law had been busy combatting horse thieves, train robbers, stage-coach bandits, and other rugged individualists.

One of these lawmen was Judge Roy Bean of west Texas. In 1882, at the urgent request of the Texas Rangers, Bean was appointed Justice of the Peace, charged with maintaining law and order in the railroad construction camps along the Southern Pacific. After the railroad was completed, Roy Bean held on to his office, and for twenty years he was the law west of the Pecos. He was a huge, gray-bearded man with a beer paunch straining over his belt. He liked Mexican sombreros, and in most of his photographs is shown with his shirt tail hanging out, a wilted bandanna knotted around his neck, a heavy gold watch chain running across a vest which is never buttoned except at the top. The Pecos was waterless country, so naturally Judge Bean drank a considerable amount of liquor and bathed only upon special occasions.

The only written law he knew was what he got out of a copy of the *Revised Statutes of Texas*, 1879 edition. He practically memorized that volume and had no use for later editions. "They sent me a new book every year or so," he once recalled, "but I used them to light fires with."

But Roy Bean gave coldblooded killers, cattle rustlers, and horse thieves no mercy. "Court's in session," he would announce, and then delivered his sentence without pausing "To be hanged by the neck until dead." As each trial ended, he would serve up cold beer all around; his court room was also his saloon.

Roy Bean may have been a great fraud in his later years, but in the early days when he was the only law west of the Pecos (a four-hundred-mile stretch of wild outlaw country), he was a fair representative of the strong-willed men who brought law and order to the West.

Continuous rough treatment from the forces of law finally discouraged most western bad men from engaging in serious crimes. Down in the southwest, however, after the male lawbreakers were fairly well thinned out, a sizable group of gunwomen arose to take the men's places. These irrepressible lady wildcats expressed themselves as freely in outlawry as other western women did in gambling and politics.

Among the more efficient of these armed females were Belle Starr, Pearl Hart, Rose of the Cimarron, Poker Alice, Cattle Annie, and Little Britches. Annie McDougal (Cattle Annie) and Jennie Metcalf (Little Britches) started their careers in their teens by selling whiskey illegally to Indians in the Osage Nation. Soon they broadened their operations to include horse thieving and cattle rustling. Occasionally they helped Bill Doolin's Wild Bunch rob a bank. A pair of U. S. Marshals finally trapped the young ladies, but Little Britches scratched her captors' faces with her long fingernails, escaped, and had to be caught again. One of the marshals shot her horse from under her.

Cattle Annie and Little Britches were sent away to a government reform school in Massachusetts. After serving her sentence, Little Britches turned to religion and died shortly afterward in a New York slum. Cattle Annie returned to Oklahoma and took up respectability.

According to legend, Rose of the Cimarron became an outlaw in order to be with her sweetheart, George (Bitter Creek) Newcombe. Newcombe robbed banks and trains with the Dalton and Doolin gangs, and Rose went along for love and excitement. The dramatic moment of her career occurred the day a posse trapped Doolin's Wild Bunch at Ingalls, Oklahoma. Rose was on the second floor of the town's only hotel when the shooting started. Realizing that her lover, Bitter Creek, was across the street without his rifle and ammunition belt, she decided to try to take them to him. But both back and front exits of the hotel were full of flying lead from the posse's guns.

Always resourceful, Rose improvised a rope from stripped bed sheets and slid to the ground through a side window. Trusting the chivalrous western marshals would not shoot an apparently unarmed woman, she concealed the rifle and belt beneath her flowing skirts and rushed across to the building where Bitter Creek was waiting. Thanks to Rose, he escaped this bloody battle but was killed two years later in another gunfight.

Like many frontier characters, Rose of the Cimarron may be more folklore than fact. Her real identity has never been satisfactorily established; some chroniclers have identified her as Rosa Dunn and Rose O'Leary, others claim she never existed at all. One of her outlaw friends revealed only that she was "a Texan born and raised," who ended her public career by marrying a homesteader and becoming the respectable mother of three children.

As the lady wildcats retreated before law and order, banditry languished in the West. Cattle and horses were secure behind barbed wire; the banks kept their money in safety vaults; the trains moved too fast for robbers; and stage coaches had all but disappeared.

But in the Teton Valley below Yellowstone Park lived an amiable fellow who had always had a yen to hold up a stagecoach. His name was Ed Trafton, and he had done time for cattle rustling in the 1880's. After his release from jail, his friends found him a job as U. S. mail carrier to keep him out of mischief.

Ed Trafton kept his eye on the stagecoaches rolling around Yellowstone Park. Automobiles were banned from the park in those days, and the stagecoaches were always filled with well-dressed tourists. These sight-seeing coaches usually moved around the park in a caravan, spaced about ten minutes apart.

On July 20, 1914, Ed Trafton and an accomplice stationed themselves near Shoshone Point and started holding up stagecoaches. They were confident nobody would shoot at them because firearms like automobiles were banned from Yellowstone. Wearing a fancy black mask and armed with a Winchester rifle, Trafton stopped 35 stagecoaches between ten in the morning and early afternoon. He would order the passengers out of each coach, line them up on the road, and then his assistant would drive the empty coach off out of sight behind a big rock outcropping.

"Cash only," Ed said politely to the tourists, and passed a big sack along each new line of victims. By the time he was finished with one group, another coach would roll around the bend, and he would hold it up. During the midst of the proceedings, one of the victims asked permission to take kodak snapshots of the next holdup. "Sure," Ed replied gallantly. He thought it was a splendid idea to have his picture made in his black mask holding up a stagecoach.

Ed Trafton took $3,000 from 165 tourists, and then decided it was time to ride away. With a friendly bow to his long line of victims, he mounted his horse and with his assistant galloped off to the north. As they rode out of the park, they cut the telegraph and telephone lines.

But law and order caught up with Ed Trafton four days later, and he served some more time in jail. His was the last stagecoach holdup in the history of the West, and it was also probably the biggest on record.

LAW, ORDER AND POLITICS

Old Ed Trafton lived until 1924. He died with his boots on, while eating an ice cream cone in a Los Angeles drugstore.

An uncommon outlaw was the Indian, but when one of these native westerners joined the fraternity, he was a rough customer. A protégé of army scout Al Sieber, the Apache Kid was a highly respected first sergeant in the Apache government scouts until he left the San Carlos Agency one day to murder an Indian who had killed his father. When Al Sieber attempted to arrest him, the Kid shot his old friend in the leg and fled the reservation.

For the next several years, the Apache Kid robbed wagon trains, rustled horses and cattle, tortured and murdered an occasional rancher who got in his way. When he wanted a squaw, he would steal one from a reservation and then leave her stranded in the desert. His name was as much feared as that of old Geronimo in Indian-fighting days.

Sheriff Glen Reynolds and a deputy at last captured the Kid with five other wanted Apaches, but en route to jail, the outlaw suddenly threw his handcuffed wrists over Reynolds' head and pinioned the sheriff's arms. While Reynolds was struggling to escape, one of the other Apaches knocked out the deputy with a pair of heavy iron handcuffs, seized his rifle, and shot the sheriff to death.

Posses were soon combing the rugged mountains and deserts of the Apache country. They caught the outlaw's five companions, but the impassive, cold-blooded Kid vanished and was never seen by white men again.

Unlike the Apache Kid, most of the Indians who lost their hunting grounds to the land-hungry settlers retreated peacefully to reservations. Some of them like old Red Cloud, the fighting Sioux leader, adopted the dress, manners, and speech of their conquerors and were more interested in making laws than breaking them. Wearing a cowboy hat, stiff white collar, and long-tailed coat, Red Cloud sometimes traveled in the east as a sort of lobbyist for laws to improve the conditions of his reservation tribesmen.

Western cavalrymen who had conquered the Indians found life tedious in a pacified West. Petty garrison duties, continual drilling, and intricate reviews for visiting generals replaced the exciting chases and battle marches. Old campaigners like General George Crook who rarely ever wore a full regulation uniform could never accustom themselves to the spit-and-polish of the West's peacetime army. One day, during a review held in his honor at a camp named for him in Nebraska, General Crook's dress trousers refused to keep company with his shoe tops, and his drawer strings broke loose, to the vast amusement of the assembled troop. "He was rather a funny spectacle, galloping down the lines on a strange and not imposing horse at the head of his staff, escort and orderlies, numbering perhaps a hundred."

In 1898, however, with the beginning of the Spanish-American War, the dormant western cavalry came to life again. But the show was stolen from the regulars by a regiment of volunteers—the First United States Volunteer Cavalry, known as the Roughriders. Organized by Theodore Roosevelt, a young New York politician and Dakota rancher, the Roughriders' regiment was made up of one thousand "good shots and good riders"—cowboys and former Indian fighters predominating. Roosevelt armed his men with six-shooters instead of sabers, trained them hard in San Antonio, and then led them to glory at San Juan Hill in Cuba. A few months later he was President, the first cowboy to reach the White House.

The last organized threat to peace and order in the West came out of Mexico when Pancho Villa and his wild-riding revolutionists crossed the border and raided Columbus, New Mexico, just before dawn of March 9, 1916. Several hundred Villistas wearing their high-crowned sombreros galloped into Columbus under cover of darkness, firing carbines and shouting, "Viva Mexico!" and "Viva Villa!" Two hundred and fifty American cavalrymen stationed in the town swarmed out of their blankets and began firing back, but the only targets were sudden flashes of carbine fire. "The raiders burned up thousands of rounds of ammunition," a cavalry lieutenant said afterwards. "Then a hotel was set afire, and this lit up the terrain so effectively that we were able to see our targets very plainly." At dawn, the raiders beat a hasty retreat, but they had killed seven American soldiers and eight civilians and left the town burning behind them.

Villa's purpose in raiding Columbus was to provoke an American cavalry pursuit into Mexico, an action which he hoped would cause the fall of the Mexican government and give the Villistas a chance to come to power. The first part of his plan worked perfectly. A troop of cavalry was mounted and hot on the trail of the raiders before they could recross the border. Under General John J. Pershing, three cavalry columns— including the famed Seventh Regiment—marched four hundred miles into Mexico in pursuit of Villa. They marched over the same type of rugged cactus-studded desert country where an earlier generation of western cavalrymen had pursued Geronimo, Cochise, and Victorio. They failed to capture Pancho Villa, but they dispersed his armies, broke his power and prestige, and restored law and order in the southwestern border country.

As the cavalry marched southward, eight thunderbirds strange to western skies flew above the dust-clouded columns, their fragile wings and struts bending and stretching, their chattering little motors breaking the silences of the hot desert land. These eight machines comprised the entire fighting air force of the United States, the First Aero Squadron, Signal Corps. By the end of the Punitive Expedition, all the planes had crashed but one, and it was so badly damaged it had to be condemned.

But the thunderbirds had made their mark on history over those unfriendly deserts of the West. General Pershing commented laconically: "One airplane is equal to a regiment of cavalry."

And there in the Apache country—where many a blue-clad soldier had fought hard to win this western land for settlement—was ended forever the old cavalry. No more would the bugle sound stable call or the charge. No more would the sergeants order "mount" or "dismount." No more would the columns go swinging away to the strains of "Garryowen" and "The Girl I Left Behind Me." The thunderbirds had erased time and space, the mysterious unknown that lay beyond horizons. The old West of the man on horseback was gone forever; the big rolling land was now the Settlers' West.

CONSTITUTION

Of The Knickerbocker Exploring Company, of the City of New York.

WE, Gentlemen of the City of New York and its vicinity, in order to form a company for the purpose of migrating to California in quest of business to better our condition, and secure for ourselves, for our families, and our friends, the blessings of an enterprise in which so many of our countrymen have so successfully engaged in, influences us in common, with others, to feel a high degree of interest, as we claim it our right and privilege to enjoy, and reap the advantages which the history of the times, and the daily events present to our knowledge, and to promote our general welfare, and secure to us an economical and safe journey to our place of destination, by augmentation, do ordain and establish this Constitution; and for the protection of each and every person enrolling as members of this Company, we do solemnly and mutually pledge to each other, our lives, our fortunes, and our sacred honors, looking with a firm reliance on Divine Providence for protection.

NAMES.		AGE.	RESIDENCE.	OCCUPATION.
CAPTAIN, John A. N. Ebbetts,	Married,	33,	New York,	Merchant.
1ST LIEUTENANT, George H. Blake,	"	24,	Troy, N. Y.,	Jeweller.
2D LIEUT., Abram A. Van Gelder,	"	26,	New York City,	Music Dealer.
TREASURER, Peter Lodewick,	Single,	28,	151, Prince St.,	Artist.
SECRETARY, James P. Burr,	Married,	41,	108 Grand St.,	Book Keeper.
Gerard Hancker,	"	33,	181, Wooster St.,	Coal Dealer.
Phineas U. Blunt,	"	39,	New York,	Soapstone worker.
B. C. Wilson,	"	30,	361, Brown St.,	Wood Turner.
Wm. F. Ford,	"	29,	New York,	Surg. Inst. Maker.
Stephen Hyde,	"	53,	163, Prince St.,	Boot&Shoe Maker.
Alx. H. Reed,	"	35,	20, Barkley St.,	Merchant.
John Flynn,	"	38,	158, Lawrence,	Cartman.
George Derrick,	Widower,	48,	404, Broadway,	Harness Maker.
James Spencer,	Married,	45,	123, Walker St.,	Artist.
Andrew Smith,	Single,	29,	Nowalk Is., Con.,	Printer.
Jessee Brush,	Married,	40,	31, Charlton St.,	Artist.
Wm. Canfield,	Married,	33,	119, Spring St.,	Jeweller.
Wm. W. Wyckoff,	Single,	26,	133, Thompson St.,	Prac. Engineer.
Hiram Green,	"	26,	New York City,	Clerk.
Barnabas Pike,	Married,	44,	"	Dry Goods' Man.
Cornelius Cornwell,	Single,	28,	"	Grocer.
John M. Hendricks,	"	23,	"	House Smith.
James E. Baker,	"	23,	67, Norfolk St.,	Mahog. Door Mak.
George Churchill,		21,	Troy, N. Y.,	Grocer.
William Moore,	"	32,	New York City,	
James Helns,	"	29,	"	Brass Worker.
Charles Churchill,	"	25,	Troy, N. Y.,	Miller.
Edgar Seabury,	Married,	28,	"	Tailor.
James H. Cooley,	"	25,	117, McDougal St.,	Painter.
Joseph Van Doren	"	28,	286, Spring St.,	Oil Merchant.
James Brown,	"	24,	50, King St.,	Hatter.
Patrick Garvey,	"	33,	38, Haumersly St.,	Tailor.
Oliver B. Oakley,	"	33,	Cor. Carm. & Bed'd,	Silver Plater.
James Lockheart,	Single,	28,	172, 6th Avenue,	Cartman.
Jas. Broadmeadow,	Married,	29,	226, Greenwich St.	Steel Manufact'r.
John Murphy,	"	29,	Harlem, N. Y.,	Stage Proprietor.
John Jones, Jr.,	Single,	28,	94, White St.,	Grocer.
Sam'l Griffiths,	Married,	26,	9th Ave. & 35th St.,	Dock Builder.
John H. Bogert,	"	26,	62, Gansvort St.,	Comb Maker.
H. M. Sturges,	Single,	24,	Weston Conn.,	Clerk.
Ira M. Allen,	Widower,	54,	New York,	Clergy. & Geol't.
Rob't W. Nevins,	Single,	41,	51, W. Wash. Place,	Merchant.
Samuel Kelly,	Married,	47,	165, Canal St.,	Exchange Brok'r.
John P. Hoyt,	"	32,	165, Canal St.,	Merchant Tailor.
James L. Byers,	Single,	20,	272, Bleecker St.,	Dry Goods Clerk.
Joel. G. Candee,	Widower,	45,	20, Park Place,	M. D.
Schuyler Hoes,	Married,	43,	Newark, N. J.,	Clergyman.
J. Alfred Kanouse,	"	24,	"	Lawyer.
Josiah H. Bruen,	"	26,	"	Farmer.
John Price,	"	29,	"	Spec. Manufact'r.
John Jackson,	Single,	17,	New York City,	
Wm. McClellan,	"	19,	"	Clerk.
T. L. Sturges,	"	25,	Wilton, Conn.,	Farmer.
James Mac Nally,	"	28,	New York City,	Iron Founder.
John Hempseed,	"	24,	333, Hudson St.,	Sad. & Har. Mak.
James M. Hutchings,	"	29,	17, Essex St.,	Grocer.
John A. Hunter,	"	29,	New York,	Surg. Inst. Maker.
Wm. R. Goulding,	Married,	42,	"	"
Samuel Y. Lum,	Single,	27,	Newark, N. J.,	Student.
Melvin S. Gardner,	"	25,	Bowdoinham, Me.,	Ship Master
E. D. Hughson,	Married,	30,	Newark, N. J.,	Baker.
E. O. Crane,	"	27,	"	Tailor.
Wm. Larison,	"	24,	"	Journalist
J. F. Hough,	Single,	20,	New York City,	Clerk.

"OUR LIVES, OUR FORTUNES, AND OUR SACRED HONORS."

Western settlers prided themselves on their independence, their freedom from restrictions common in older societies. Group organization, however, was necessary for survival, and before the settlers reached their destinations they usually found themselves bound together by written constitutions such as this one of the Knickerbocker Exploring Company of the City of New York, organized for the purpose of migrating to California.

SAN FRANCISCO UNION MEETING

By the time of the Civil War, the West was sufficiently organized to take sides in the conflict. On May 11, 1861, along San Francisco's Market Street, a group of Union sympathizers rallied as shown around the bannered words of Daniel Webster: "The Union, the Whole Union, and Nothing But the Union." A few days later, California voted to support the Union, and all the West followed its example.

"SUSPENDED SENTENCE" (on facing page, top)

But the first settlements, being under loose territorial control, had neither laws nor officers for enforcement. Although crime was generally unknown in the homesteading country, mining towns often became so lawless that the only cure was "a short cord and a good drop." In this photograph, virtually the entire population of the Leadville, Colorado, area is shown dressed up in their best clothing to witness a double hanging.

WESTERN WOMEN BREAK LOOSE: CALAMITY JANE (on facing page, bottom)

During the wild years when society in the West was without "forms and ceremonies," the women who had crossed the plains and mountains gradually discovered that they were a free sex. Western women broke loose from centuries of law and order, starting a revolution which is still spreading around the world. Arch-rebel in this western revolt was Calamity Jane, shown on a sidewalk in Gilt Edge, Montana, with a male conspirator who looks very much like Teddy Blue, the immortal trail driver.

WYOMING'S VOTERS IN SKIRTS

In Wyoming Territory, December 10, 1869, for the first time anywhere, women were invested with "all the political rights, duties, franchises, and responsibilities of male citizens." And since that day, Wyoming's male citizens have been arguing among themselves as to why and how this remarkable thing ever came about. Whatever the reasons, both political parties immediately began vying with each other for support from the new voters, providing fine horse carriages to transport them to the polls.

YUMA INDIANS: ON ELECTION DAY THEIR NAMES WERE IRISH

Western politicians wanted everybody to vote, including on certain occasions the franchise-less Indians. "The politicians would bring a string of Yuma Indians up to vote," recalled an Arizona settler of the 1870's. "They wore nothing but a breech-cloth and perhaps a stove-pipe hat, and held their already marked tickets in their hand. When a clerk would ask an Indian his name he would say 'Sullivan' or 'Malony' or any other good Irish name he had been drilled in saying."

NATIONAL GRANGE MEETING (below)

The settlers' abilities for ready organization were demonstrated during the dark years following the Panic of 1873. They rushed by thousands to form units of the Patrons of Husbandry, or National Grange. Western farmers were angry over the high prices they had to pay for things they had to buy and the low prices they received for things they had to sell. Through united action in the Grange, they hoped to improve their low economic condition.

THE SONGS OF CAROLINE ARABELLA HALL

Western women, being western women, became members of the Grange along with their men. At first there was strong opposition from the male founders, but Miss Caroline Arabella Hall of Minnesota traveled to Washington headquarters and insisted on women being admitted, even though the Grange was a secret society. And before long, all over the West the settlers and their wives were attending meetings and singing songs together out of a Grange song book compiled by Miss Caroline Arabella Hall.

FARMERS' ALLIANCE OF TEXAS (above)

By the late 1870's, enthusiasm for the Grange was beginning to wane. The organization's leaders shied away from politics and seemed to be making no headway with their program to better the lot of the western farmers. About this time, far out in Lampasas County, Texas, a group of settlers organized the Texas Alliance, a political movement which spread through the West and soon became the Farmers' Alliance.

SOCKLESS JERRY SIMPSON

"The Grange was full of poetry," said Jerry Simpson of Kansas, "the Alliance was full of politics." And Jerry Simpson *(left)* was a natural-born frontier politician. Running for office on the Alliance ticket against a wealthy lawyer, he described his opponent as a "prince in silk stockings." The newspapers immediately labeled Jerry Simpson as the "Sockless Socrates," and for the remainder of his career he was Sockless Jerry Simpson.

CAMPAIGNING IN KANSAS

The dynamic Farmers' Alliance drew into its ranks all the voices of dissent in the West. "The campaign of 1890 was a good deal more than a political campaign," commented the Kansas City *Times.* "It was a religious revival, a crusade." Above is shown the eloquent Sockless Jerry Simpson campaigning in Kansas.

MARY E. LEASE: "MY TONGUE IS LOOSE AT BOTH ENDS AND HUNG ON A SWIVEL"

Foremost among the western women who enrolled in this revolt of the settlers was Mary Elizabeth Lease *(right)*. "The people are at bay," she cried. "Let the bloodhounds of money who have dogged us thus far beware. What the farmers need is to *raise less corn and more hell!*" Wearing her high-collared black dress which became a sort of trademark, Mary Lease made 161 speeches during the campaign of 1890, admitting frankly: "My tongue is loose at both ends and hung on a swivel."

THE POPULIST UPRISING

When the ballots were counted after the elections of 1890, the nation was startled by the power of the settlers' revolt; the Alliance won control in several states west of the Mississippi. By 1892, the movement had become a national political party—the People's Party, or the Populists. *Above* is a group of Populists gathered for a local convention in Nebraska; the faces of these western plainsmen reflect the resolute mood of the times.

WILLIAM ALFRED PEFFER
AND BEARD (right)

Among western leaders campaigning for the Populists in that dramatic political year of 1892 was Senator William Alfred Peffer of Kansas. "Formerly the man who lost his farm could go west," said he. "Now there is no longer any west to go to. Now they have to fight for their homes instead of making new." Even in a day when beards were common, Senator Peffer's facial adornment attracted national attention. "He is not obliged to spend money for a Christmas tree," one newspaper commented. "He simply puts glass balls, small candles, strings of popcorn and cornucopias in his magnificent whiskers and there you are."

JAMES B. WEAVER,
CANDIDATE FOR PRESIDENT

In Omaha, July 4, 1892, the People's Party nominated General James B. Weaver of Iowa *(left)* to run for President against the candidates of the two old parties.

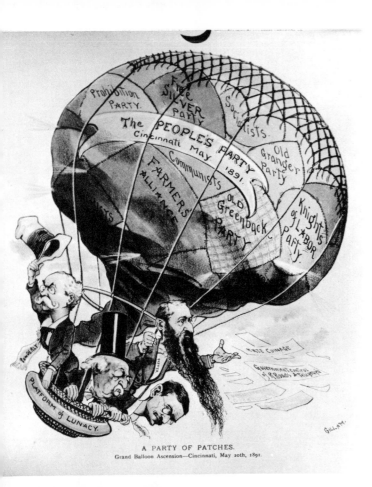

A PARTY OF PATCHES.
Grand Balloon Ascension—Cincinnati, May 20th, 1891.

"A PARTY OF PATCHES"

The noisy campaigning of the Populists was heard across the nation. Here is a typical cartoon of the times, depicting People's Party leaders adrift in a patched balloon. Sockless Jerry Simpson is leaning far out of the basket, and Senator Peffer's beard is blowing in the wind. The presidential election of 1892 was an unorthodox affair, with voters crossing party lines in all directions. When it was over, the Populists were victorious only in the West, while the rest of the country elected Grover Cleveland and a Democratic government.

"WAR TIMES IN TOPEKA"

In Kansas the Populists won their most spectacular victories, but there was a dispute with the Republicans over control of one branch of the legislature. Both sides threatened violence, and the newly elected Populist governor called out the militia. Gatling guns rolled upon the capitol grounds in Topeka (above), but the weapons were harmless because some one had stolen the operating cranks.

CARL (OLD GREASY) BROWNE

Free silver became a popular panacea for relieving the West's economic plight, and in the summer of 1893 a convention of silver advocates gathered in Chicago. One of the more flamboyant delegates was Carl Browne of California *(above)*; his friends called him "Old Greasy" because he seldom took time to bathe. During the Free Silver convention, Browne convinced another delegate, mild-mannered Jacob Coxey of Ohio, that an army of a million westerners was ready to march on Washington. So was born the idea of Coxey's Army.

ARMED PEACE *(on facing page, top)*

A blizzard interrupted action for several hours, and when the weather cleared the Populists agreed to leave the dispute to the courts for settlement. Sergeants-at-arms moved in to keep the peace, posing for this photograph. The courts ruled in favor of the Republicans, and from that time the People's Party began its decline.

TURMOIL IN DENVER *(on facing page, bottom)*

In spite of the Populists' victories, more unrest came to the West with the money panic of 1893. Silver prices dropped sharply, forcing mines to close. Banks shut their doors. Thousands of unemployed drifted into Denver, and when Governor "Bloody Bridles" Waite attempted to provide food and shelter, he became involved in a dispute with Denver city officials. Rioting followed, cannon were aimed at the City Hall, and federal troops had to be rushed in to restore order.

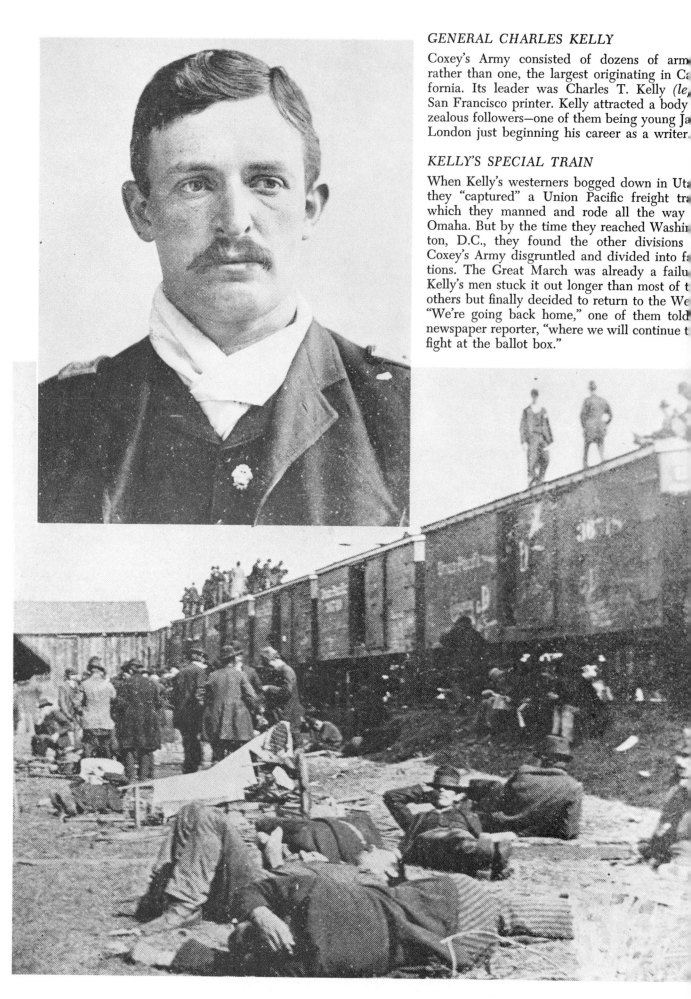

GENERAL CHARLES KELLY

Coxey's Army consisted of dozens of arm[ies] rather than one, the largest originating in Ca[li]fornia. Its leader was Charles T. Kelly *(le[ft])* San Francisco printer. Kelly attracted a body [of] zealous followers—one of them being young Ja[ck] London just beginning his career as a writer.

KELLY'S SPECIAL TRAIN

When Kelly's westerners bogged down in Ut[ah] they "captured" a Union Pacific freight tr[ain] which they manned and rode all the way [to] Omaha. But by the time they reached Washi[ng]ton, D.C., they found the other divisions [of] Coxey's Army disgruntled and divided into f[ac]tions. The Great March was already a failu[re]. Kelly's men stuck it out longer than most of t[he] others but finally decided to return to the We[st]. "We're going back home," one of them told [a] newspaper reporter, "where we will continue t[he] fight at the ballot box."

SILVER KNIGHT OF THE WEST

Meanwhile in Nebraska, 34-year-old William Jennings Bryan was laying plans to insure that his name would be on the next presidential ballot as the choice of the rebellious westerners. Borrowing practically all the Populists' 1892 platform, with emphasis on Free Silver, Bryan charged into the Chicago Democratic Convention of 1896, captured it with his "Cross of Gold" speech, and won the presidential nomination.

ELUSIVENESS OF VICTORY

"Little Billy Bryan Chasing Butterflies," was the caption under this composite photograph-cartoon of 1896. The Silver Knight campaigned everywhere, averaging thirty speeches every day. He failed to capture his butterfly, but he came very close. 20,000 votes more would have taken him into the White House. Bryan was to make two more tries for the presidency, but the West along with the rest of the country entered upon a period of prosperity with the coming of the new century. Organized protests were no longer popular.

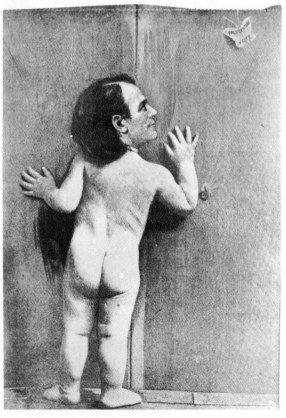

ROY BEAN: "COURT'S IN SESSION"

While western politicians were making history—if not winning elections—the appointed keepers of the law had been busy combatting rustlers, horse thieves, bandits, and other rugged individualists. One of these lawmen was Judge Roy Bean of west Texas, shown *above* wearing his Mexican sombrero while he dispenses beer and justice to a horse thief on the porch of his combination courtroom and saloon.

WESTERN SHERIFF AT WORK

The sheriff—lonely, proud, corrupt, deadly, cowardly, or brave—has been well preserved in the annals of the American West. In actuality, western sheriffs spent as much time riding swivel chairs before rolltop desks as they did on horses leading posses. During the gold rush heyday of Virginia City, Nevada, the local sheriff posed for a photo in his office, as shown *above*. The bottle in the closet contains ink.

CATTLE ANNIE AND LITTLE BRITCHES

In some parts of the West, gunwomen gave the sheriffs more trouble than the gunmen. These irrepressible lady wildcats expressed themselves as freely in outlawry as other women did in gambling and politics. Cattle Annie (Annie McDougal) and Little Britches (Jennie Metcalf) peddled whiskey to Oklahoma Indians, stole horses, rustled cattle, and occasionally robbed a bank. After considerable gunfire and face-scratching, they were at last taken into custody and shipped east to a reform school. Little Britches later turned to religion, died in a New York slum. Cattle Annie returned to Oklahoma to take up respectability.

ROSE OF THE CIMARRON

One of the more mysterious women outlaws was Rose of the Cimarron, identified as Rosa Dun or Rose O'Leary (right). Some modern investigators claim she never existed, but the legend persists that Rose became an outlaw in order to be with her sweetheart, George (Bitter Creek) Newcombe. One of the controversial incidents of her outlaw career is the gunfight at Ingalls, Oklahoma, during which she is said to have crossed a street full of flying lead, a rifle concealed beneath her flowing skirts. With this rifle her lover made his escape. Rose later married a homesteader and settled down to raise a family.

THE FRIENDLY BANDIT
OF YELLOWSTONE PARK

After the lady wildcats retreated before law and order, banditry languished in the West. But the last stagecoach robbery was not pulled off until July 20, 1914, on the eve of World War I. The scene was Yellowstone Park where automobiles were then forbidden, and tourists viewed the sights from fancy yellow stagecoaches. The bandit was Ed Trafton (*above*), a friendly sort of road agent. He stopped thirty-five coaches in succession, an accomplice leading each one off out of view before the next one came along. Trafton permitted his victims to take kodak snapshots of the proceedings. After collecting $3,000 in cash, he and his pal cut the telegraph lines and galloped away to the north. The law caught up with them four days later.

RED CLOUD AFTER THE WARS

Unlike the Apache Kid, most reservation Indians were law-abiding. Some of them like old Red Cloud, the fighting Sioux leader, were more interested in making laws than breaking them. Wearing his tall hat, stiff collar, long-tailed coat, and a haircut shorter than that of his friend, Colonel Charles Jordan (*right*), Red Cloud sometimes traveled in the east as a sort of lobbyist for laws to improve the conditions of his people.

THE APACHE KID

An uncommon sort of outlaw was the Indian, but when one of these native westerners turned *bandido* he was a rough customer. The Apache Kid began his bloody career with a murder; then shot army scout Al Sieber in the leg when the latter attempted to arrest him. For the next several years, the Kid was the terror of the southwestern border country, his name as much feared as that of old Geronimo in Indian-fighting days.

UNEMPLOYED SCOUT

Hundreds of civilian army scouts found themselves without employment in a West of law and order. After years of danger and excitement, the chase had ended. Scouts despised farming as heartily as did most Indians, and many of them wasted out their lives around army posts and reservations. Like Frank Grouard *(above)*, they took to drink, grew fat and lazy, occasionally earned a few pennies posing for traveling stereo photographers.

FIELD EXERCISES

Soldiers also found life tedious in a pacified West. Petty garrison duties, continual drilling, and intricate reviews for visiting generals replaced the exciting marches and chases after Indians. As often as possible, the old-timers invented excuses to escape the confines of their garrisons, and rode away to perform field exercises as shown in this photograph.

TEDDY ROOSEVELT
AND HIS ROUGH RIDERS

The dormant western cavalry came to life in 1898 with the beginning of the Spanish-American War. Theodore Roosevelt, young New York politician and Dakota rancher, organized the Rough Riders—a regiment of one thousand "good shots and good riders," with cowboys, army scouts, and Indian fighters predominating. Roosevelt armed his men with six-shooters instead of sabers, led them to glory at San Juan Hill, and a few months later he was President—the first cowboy to reach the White House.

PANCHO VILLA

The last organized threat to peace and order in the West came out of Mexico when Pancho Villa *(right)* and his wild-riding revolutionaries crossed the border and raided Columbus, New Mexico, just before dawn of March 9, 1916.

COLUMBUS, NEW MEXICO, AFTER THE RAID

Under cover of darkness, several hundred Villistas galloped into Columbus, firing carbines and shouting, "Viva Villa!" Stationed in the town were 250 U. S. cavalrymen; they rolled out of their blankets and began firing back. At dawn the raiders beat a hasty retreat, but they left behind them fifteen dead American citizens and a burning town. *Above* is shown burned-out section of Columbus, photographed the morning after the raid.

THE WEST'S LAST GREAT CAVALRY MARCH

Villa's purpose in raiding Columbus was to provoke the United States Army into an invasion of Mexico and thus give him a chance to seize power in the Mexican government. The first part of his plan worked perfectly. Three columns of United States cavalry marched in pursuit over the same desert country where earlier generations of horse soldiers had pursued Apaches. They failed to capture Pancho Villa, but they dispersed his armies and restored law and order along the southwestern border.

HAIL AND FAREWELL!

As the cavalry marched southward, eight chattering thunderbirds strange to western skies flew above the dust-clouded columns. These eight machines comprised the entire fighting air force of the United States, but they made their mark on history—erasing time and space and the mysterious unknown that lay beyond the horseman's horizon. The old wild West was gone forever, the big rolling land was now the settlers' West. (In photograph *above* Major H. A. Dargue is standing beside his airplane after landing it at Chihuahua. Villista sympathizers had rushed forward, stoning him and his plane, but they ceased their hostilities when a Mexican photographer arrived to take pictures.)

BIBLIOGRAPHY

Aeschbacher, W. D., "Development of cattle raising in the Sand Hills." *Nebraska History,* Vol. 28, pp. 41-64 (1947).

Allen, Albert H., *Dakota Imprints, 1858-1889.* R. R. Bowker Co., New York, 1947.

Allsopp, Fred W., *History of the Arkansas Press.* Parke-Harper, Little Rock, 1922.

Applegate, Oliver C., Papers, 1847-1870. (Manuscript. University of Oregon Library).

Bancroft, Hubert H., *History of Nevada, Colorado and Wyoming.* San Francisco, 1890.

———, *History of Washington, Idaho, and Montana.* San Francisco, 1890.

Barnes, Will C., "Col. James Harvey McClintock, pioneer, historian, soldier and citizen." *Arizona Historical Review,* Vol. 6, no. 1, pp. 67-74 (January 1935).

Bennett, Estelline, *Old Deadwood Days.* New York, 1928.

Binns, Archie, *Northwest Gateway.* Doubleday, Doran, New York, 1941.

Blake, Henry N., "The first newspaper of Montana." Historical Society of Montana, *Contributions,* Vol. 5, pp. 253-273 (1904).

Boatright, Mody C., and Day, Donald, *Backwoods to Border* (Texas Folklore Society, Publication No. 18). Austin, 1943.

Botkin, Theodosius, "Among the sovereign squats." Kansas State Historical Society, *Transactions,* Vol. 7, pp. 418-441 (1902).

Branch, Edgar M., *The Literary Apprenticeship of Mark Twain.* University of Illinois Press, Urbana, 1950.

Brandon, C. Watt, "Building a town on Wyoming's last frontier." *Annals of Wyoming,* Vol. 22, pp. 27-46 (1950).

Brecht, Frederick G., "Reminiscences." *Arizona Historical Review,* Vol. 6, no. 1, pp. 85-86 (January 1935).

Britt, Albert, "Ride 'im, cowboy!" *Outlook,* Vol. 135, pp. 136-139 (1923).

Britton, Wiley, *Pioneer Life in Southwest Missouri.* Smith-Grieves Co., Kansas City, Missouri, 1929.

Brown, Dee, and Schmitt, Martin F., *Trail Driving Days.* Charles Scribner's Sons, New York, 1952.

Brownsville (Nebraska) *Advertiser,* June 6 and October 18, 1856, as quoted in *Nebraska History,* Vol. 26, pp. 240, 242 (1945).

Bryan, O. S., "An early Dakota camp meeting." *South Dakota Historical Collections,* Vol. 20, pp. 281-298 (1940).

Buchanan, John R., "The great railroad migration into northern Nebraska." Nebraska State Historical Society, *Proceedings,* Vol. 15, pp. 25-34 (1907).

Buck, Solon J., *The Agrarian Crusade, a Chronicle of the Farmer in Politics.* Yale University Press, New Haven, 1921.

Burdick, Usher L., "Recollections and reminiscences of Graham's Island." *North Dakota History,* Vol. 16, pp. 5-29; 165-191 (1949).

Buxbaum, Katherine, "A rural literary society." *Palimpsest,* Vol. 21, pp. 23-30 (1940).

"Camel breeding in Texas." *National Live-Stock Journal,* Vol. 9, p. 299 (1878).

Case, Victoria, *We Called It Culture.* Doubleday, Garden City, N. Y., 1948.

Casey, Robert J., *Pioneer Railroad.* Whittlesey House, New York, 1948.

Chatterton, Fenimore, "A unique campaign." *Annals of Wyoming,* Vol. 19, pp. 32-38 (1947).

Chittenden, Hiram M., *The American Fur Trade of the Far West.* F. P. Harper, New York, 1902.

Clancy, Foghorn, *My Fifty Years in Rodeo.* Naylor Co., San Antonio, 1952.

———, "Rodeo progress." *Hoofs and Horns,* Vol. 23, no. 2, p. 17 (August 1953).

Clarke, Robert D., *The Works of Sitting Bull.* Knight and Leonard, Chicago, 1878.

Clemens, Samuel L., *Roughing It.* Hartford, Conn., 1891.

Cody, William F., *Buffalo Bill's Own Story of His Life and Deeds.* Homewood Press, Chicago, 1917.

Coffin, William H., "Settlement of the Friends in Kansas." Kansas State Historical Society, *Transactions,* Vol. 7, pp. 322-361 (1902).

Coletta, Paolo E., "The youth of William Jennings Bryan—beginnings of a Christian statesman." *Nebraska History,* Vol. 31, pp. 1-24 (1950).

Collings, Ellsworth, and England, Alma M., *The 101 Ranch.* University of Oklahoma Press, Norman, 1937.

Cooke, Jay & Co., *The Northern Pacific Railroad.* Philadelphia, 1871.

Cox, W. W., "Reminiscences of early days in Nebraska." Nebraska Historical Society, *Transactions,* Vol. 5, pp. 63-81 (1893).

Coyle, James, "Letter to Arizona Pioneers Historical Society." *Arizona Historical Review,* Vol. 6, no. 5, p. 87 (July 1935).

Crawford, Captain Jack, *Lariattes.* William A. Bell, Sigourney, Iowa, 1904.

——, *The Poet Scout, a Book of Song and Story.* Funk and Wagnalls, New York, 1886.

Crawford, Medorem, Letters, 1846-1860. (Manuscript, University of Oregon Library).

Crawford, Nelson Antrim, "The making of a hero." *Kansas Magazine,* pp. 1-5 (1949).

Creigh, Thomas Alfred. "From Nebraska City to Montana, 1866"; diary edited by James C. Olson. *Nebraska History,* Vol. 29, pp. 208-237 (1948).

Crofutt, George, *Crofutt's New Overland Tourist and Pacific Coast Guide.* Chicago, 1878.

Croke, James, Letters, 1854. (Manuscript, University of Oregon Library).

Crook, George, *General George Crook.* University of Oklahoma Press, Norman, 1946.

Cummins, Henry, Letters, 1859-1862. (Manuscript, University of Oregon Library).

Dale, Edward E., "The social homesteader." *Nebraska History,* Vol. 25, pp. 155-171 (1944).

——, "Wood and water: twin problems of the prairie plains." *Nebraska History,* Vol. 29, pp. 87-104 (1948).

Davidson, Jay Brownlee, *Farm Machinery and Farm Motors.* Orange Judd Co., New York, 1908.

Delano, Alonzo, *Pen-knife Sketches.* Grabhorn Press, San Francisco, 1934.

Denhardt, Robert M., *The Horse of the Americas.* University of Oklahoma Press, Norman, 1948.

De Voto, Bernard, *Mark Twain's America.* Little, Brown, Boston, 1932.

Dick, Everett N., *The Sod-house Frontier.* D. Appleton-Century, New York, 1937.

Dickinson County Chronicle (Abilene, Kansas), June 7, 1878, as quoted in *Kansas Historical Quarterly,* Vol. 14, p. 233 (1946).

——, June 28, 1878, as quoted in *Kansas Historical Quarterly,* Vol. 12, p. 325 (1943).

Diggs, Annie L., *The Story of Jerry Simpson.* Wichita, Kansas, 1908.

——, "Women in the Alliance movement." *Arena,* Vol. 6, pp. 160-179 (1892).

Dimsdale, Thomas J., *The Vigilantes of Montana.* University of Oklahoma Press, Norman, 1953.

Dobie, J. Frank, *Guide to Life and Literature of the Southwest.* Southern Methodist University Press, Dallas, 1952.

Dodd, E. P., Scrapbook history. (Manuscript. University of Oregon Library).

Dolbee, Cora, "The Fourth of July in early Kansas." *Kansas Historical Quarterly,* Vol. 11, pp. 130-172 (1942).

Doran, Thomas F., "Kansas sixty years ago." Kansas State Historical Society, *Collections,* Vol. 15, pp. 482-501 (1923).

Dorson, Richard M., *Davy Crockett, American Comic Legend.* Rockland Editions, New York, 1939.

Driggs, Benjamin W., *History of Teton Valley.* Caxton Printers, Caldwell, Idaho, 1926.

Dunn, Nora G., "Reminiscences of fourscore years and eight." *Annals of Wyoming,* Vol. 19, pp. 125-135 (1947).

Duval, John C., *Adventures of Big-Foot Wallace.* J. W. Burke and Co., Macon, Ga., 1885.

——, *Early Times in Texas.* H. P. N. Gammel and Co., Austin, 1892.

Dykes, J. C., "Dime-novel Texas; or, the subliterature of the Lone Star State." *Southwestern Historical Quarterly,* Vol. 49, pp. 327-340 (1946).

Ellis, William T., *Memories.* J. H. Nash, Eugene, Oregon, 1939.

Eureka (Kansas) *Herald,* May 10, 1877, as quoted in *Kansas Historical Quarterly,* Vol. 11, p. 96 (1942).

Expeditions of Capt. Jas. L. Fisk to the gold mines of Idaho and Montana, 1864-1866. *North Dakota State Historical Collections,* Vol. 2, pp. 421-461 (1908).

Fitzpatrick, Lilian, *Nebraska Place Names.* University of Nebraska, Lincoln, 1925.

Fox, John J., "The far West in the 80's," edited by T. A. Larson. *Annals of Wyoming,* Vol. 21, pp. 3-87 (1949).

Frantz, Joe B., "Moses Lapham: his life and selected correspondence." *Southwestern Historical Quarterly,* Vol. 54, pp. 324-332; 462-475 (1950-1951).

Furlong, Charles W., *Let 'er Buck, a Story of the Passing of the Old West.* G. P. Putnam's Sons, New York, 1923.

Gallego, Hilario, "Reminiscences of an Arizona pioneer." *Arizona Historical Review*, Vol. 6, no. 1, pp. 75-81 (January 1935).

Gard, Wayne, "The fence-cutters." *Southwestern Historical Quarterly*, Vol. 51, pp. 1-15 (1947).

——, *Frontier Justice.* University of Oklahoma Press, Norman, 1949.

Gardner, Charles M., *The Grange—Friend of the Farmer.* National Grange, Washington, D. C., 1949.

Garland, Hamlin, *A Son of the Middle Border.* Macmillan, New York, 1925.

Giles, Barney M., "Early military aviation in Texas." *Southwestern Historical Quarterly*, Vol. 54, pp. 143-158 (1950).

Goldberg, Isaac, "Reminiscences." *Arizona Historical Review*, Vol. 6, no. 2, pp. 74-82 (April 1935).

Greeley, Horace, *An Overland Journey from New York to San Francisco.* New York, 1860.

Hadley, James A., "A royal buffalo hunt." Kansas State Historical Society, *Transactions*, Vol. 10, pp. 564-580 (1908).

Hafen, Le Roy R., and Hafen, Ann W., *Colorado.* Old West Publishing Co., Denver, 1945.

Hall, Caroline Arabella, *Songs for the Grange, Set to Music and Dedicated to the Order of Patrons of Husbandry in the United States.* J. A. Wagenseller, Philadelphia, 1873.

Hansen, George W., "A tragedy of the Oregon Trail." Nebraska State Historical Society, *Transactions*, Vol. 17, pp. 110-126 (1913).

Harlow, Alvin F., *Old Waybills.* D. Appleton-Century, New York, 1934.

Harrington, W. P., "The Populist Party in Kansas." Kansas State Historical Society, *Collections*, Vol. 16, pp. 403-450 (1923-1925).

Hibben, Paxton, *The Peerless Leader, William Jennings Bryan.* Farrar and Rinehart, New York, 1929.

Hickman, Ervin, "Fredricksburg, Texas; 100 years of progress." *Cattleman*, Vol. 33, pp. 29-30, 110-112 (January 1947).

Hicks, John D., *The Populist Revolt.* University of Minnesota Press, Minneapolis, 1931.

Hill City (Kansas) *New Era*, June 18, 1908; as quoted in *Kansas Historical Quarterly*, Vol. 19, pp. 216-217 (1951).

Historical Records Survey. *Checklist of Kansas Imprints, 1854-1876.* Topeka, Kansas, 1939.

Hoeltje, Hubert H., "The apostle of the sunflower in the state of the tall corn." *Palimpsest*, Vol. 18, pp. 186-211 (1937).

Holbrook, Stewart, *Holy Old Mackinaw.* Macmillan, New York, 1938.

Horton, James C., "Peter D. Ridenour and George W. Baker." Kansas State Historical Society, *Transactions*, Vol. 10, pp. 589-621 (1908).

Hough, Emerson, "Texas transformed." *Putnam's Magazine*, Vol. 7, pp. 200-207 (November 1909).

House, Boyce, "Spindletop." *Southwestern Historical Quarterly*, Vol. 50, pp. 36-43 (1946).

Howe, Edgar, *Plain People.* Dodd, Mead, New York, 1929.

Howe, George F., *Chester A. Arthur.* Dodd, Mead, New York, 1934.

Humphrey, Seth K., *Following the Prairie Frontier.* University of Minnesota Press, Minneapolis, 1931.

Hunt, Frazier, and Hunt, Robert, *Horses and Heroes.* Charles Scribner's Sons, New York, 1949.

Hunter, J. Marvin, and Rose, Noah H., *The Album of Gunfighters.* Bandera, Texas, 1951.

Interstate Agricultural Convention, 1880. *Proceedings.* Springfield, Illinois, 1881.

Irwin, Clark, "Early settlers en route." Nebraska State Historical Society, *Transactions*, Vol. 3, pp. 191-200 (1892).

Jack, Frances E., "P. E. O. beginnings." *Palimpsest*, Vol. 23, pp. 85-98 (1942).

Jackson, Joseph Henry, *Anybody's Gold.* Appleton-Century, New York, 1941.

Jeffries, Charlie, "Reminiscences of Sour Lake." *Southwestern Historical Quarterly*, Vol. 50, pp. 25-35 (1946).

Jennewein, J. Leonard, *Calamity Jane of the Western Trails.* Dakota Books, Huron, South Dakota, 1953.

Jocelyn, Stephen P., *Mostly Alkali.* Caxton Printers, Caldwell, Idaho, 1953.

Johannsen, Albert, *The House of Beadle and Adams and its Dime and Nickel Novels; the Story of a Vanished Literature.* University of Oklahoma Press, Norman, 1950.

Johnson, Walter, "Politics in the midwest." *Nebraska History*, Vol. 32, pp. 1-17 (1951).

Johnson, Willard D., "The high plains and their utilization." U. S. Geological Survey, *Twenty-first Annual Report*, Pt. 4, pp. 609-741 (1899-1900).

Jones, Alf D., "Omaha's early days." Nebraska State Historical Society, *Transactions*, Vol. 4, pp. 152-154 (1892).

Junction City (Kansas) Union, July 27, 1867, as quoted in *Kansas Historical Quarterly*, Vol. 16, p. 411 (1948).

Junction City (Kansas) Union, July 8, 1871, as quoted in *Kansas Historical Quarterly*, Vol. 10, pp. 329-330 (1941).

Kansas Chief (White Cloud), August 6, 1857, as quoted in *Kansas Historical Quarterly*, Vol. 20, p. 298 (1952).

———, January 5, 1860, as quoted in *Kansas Historical Quarterly*, Vol. 14, p. 447 (1946).

Kansas Daily Commonwealth (Topeka), June 16, 1872, as quoted in *Kansas Historical Quarterly*, Vol. 11, p. 402 (1942).

Kautz, August V., "From Missouri to Oregon in 1860." *Pacific Northwest Quarterly*, Vol. 37, pp. 193-230 (1946).

Keithley, Ralph, *Buckey O'Neill*. Caxton Printers, Caldwell, Idaho, 1949.

Kendall, Jane R., "History of Fort Francis E. Warren." *Annals of Wyoming*, Vol. 18, pp. 3-66 (1946).

King, Frank M., *Pioneer Western Empire Builders*. Pasadena, Calif., 1946.

Kinsley (Kansas) Graphic, January 17, 1880, as quoted in *Kansas Historical Quarterly*, Vol. 18, p. 429 (1950).

Kiowa (Kansas) Herald, January 8, 1885, as quoted in *Kansas Historical Quarterly*, Vol. 17, p. 302 (1949).

Kipling, Rudyard, *American Notes*. G. Munro's Sons, New York, 1896.

Koller, Joe, "Indian rodeos in the Dakotas." *Hoofs and Horns*, Vol. 22, p. 14 (June 1953).

Lakin (Kansas) Eagle, August 27, 1879, as quoted in *Kansas Historical Quarterly*, Vol. 6, pp. 104-105 (1937).

Lamb, Ted, "Trick riding." *Hoofs and Horns*, Vol. 22, p. 15 (March 1953).

"Laramie City, a review for 1868-1869," reprinted from Laramie Weekly *Sentinel*, May 5, 1883. *Annals of Wyoming*, Vol. 15, pp. 391-402 (1943).

Larson, Agnes M., *History of the White Pine Industry in Minnesota*. University of Minnesota Press, Minneapolis, 1949.

Levinson, Harry, "Mary Elizabeth Lease: prairie radical." *Kansas Magazine*, pp. 18-24 (1948).

Lewis, Lloyd, and Pargellis, Stanley, *Granger Country, a Pictorial Social History of the Burlington Railroad*. Little, Brown, Boston, 1949.

Lomax, Susan F., "A trip to Texas," edited by John A. Lomax. *Southwestern Historical Quarterly*, Vol. 48, pp. 254-261 (1944).

Long, J. C., *Bryan the Great Commoner*. Appleton, New York, 1928.

Lutrell, Estelle, "Arizona's frontier press." *Arizona Historical Review*, Vol. 6, pp. 14-26 (1935).

McArthur, Lewis A., *Oregon Geographic Names*. Binfords and Mort, Portland, Oregon, 1944.

McCampbell, C. W., "W. E. Campbell, pioneer Kansas livestockman." *Kansas Historical Quarterly*, Vol. 16, pp. 245-273 (1948).

McCann, Leo P., "Ride 'im, cowboy!" *Sunset Magazine*, Vol. 59, pp. 18-20, 62 (September 1927).

McComas, Evans, Diary, 1864-1866. (Manuscript. University of Oregon Library).

McMurry, Donald L., *Coxey's Army*. Little, Brown, Boston, 1929.

McMurtrie, Douglas C., *Oregon Imprints, 1847-1870*. University of Oregon Press, Eugene, 1950.

McNeal, Thomas A., "Southwestern Kansas." Kansas State Historical Society, *Transactions*, Vol. 7, pp. 90-95 (1902).

Mahnken, Norbert R., "William Jennings Bryan in Oklahoma." *Nebraska History*, Vol. 31, pp. 247-274 (1950).

Major, Mabel, *Southwest Heritage*. University of New Mexico Press, Albuquerque, 1938.

Malin, James C., *Dust storms, 1850-1900*. Reprint from *Kansas Historical Quarterly*, 1946.

Martin, George W., "A chapter from the archives." Kansas State Historical Society, *Collections*, Vol. 12, pp. 259-375 (1912).

Meeker, Ezra, *Ventures and adventures of Ezra Meeker*. Rainier Publishing Co., Seattle, 1908.

Monaghan, Jay, *The Great Rascal, the Life and Adventures of Ned Buntline*. Little, Brown, Boston, 1952.

Mott, Frank L., *American Journalism*. Macmillan, New York, 1950.

Mowry, Sylvester, Letters, 1855-1856. (Manuscript. University of Oregon Library).

Munro, J. A., "Grasshopper outbreaks in North Dakota, 1808-1948." *North Dakota History*, Vol. 16, pp. 143-164 (1949).

Munson, Lyman E., "Pioneer life in Montana." Historical Society of Montana, *Contributions*, Vol. 5, pp. 200-234 (1904).

Nye, Edgar Wilson, *Nye and Riley's Railway Guide*. Dearborn Pub. Co., Chicago, 1888.

Orchard, Hugh, *Old Orchard Farm*. Iowa State College Press, Ames, 1952.

Owen, Mary A., "Social customs and usages in Missouri during the last century." *Missouri Historical Review*, Vol. 15, pp. 176-190 (1920).

Paine, Bayard H., *Pioneers, Indians and Buffaloes*. Curtis Enterprise, Curtis, Nebraska, 1935.

Palmer, Alma B., "Fire! fire! fire!" *Nebraska History*, Vol. 33, pp. 180-185 (1952).

Palmer, Joel, *Journal of Travels over the Rocky Mountains*. A. H. Clark Co., Cleveland, 1906.

Pearson, Edmund, *Dime Novels; or, Following an Old Trail in Popular Literature*. Little, Brown, Boston, 1929.

Peterson, Harold F., "Some colonization projects of the Northern Pacific Railroad." *Minnesota History*, Vol. 10, pp. 127-144 (1929).

"Pioneering in Waubausee county." Kansas State Historical Society, *Transactions*, Vol. 11, pp. 594-613 (1910).

"The Pioneers." *Palimpsest*, Vol. 8, pp. 1-56 (1927).

Platt, M. F., "Reminiscences of early days in Nebraska." Nebraska Historical Society, *Transactions*, Vol. 4, pp. 87-95 (1892).

Porter, Robert P., *The West: from the Census of 1880*. Rand, McNally & Co., Chicago, 1882.

Porter, Willard H., "Rope, trip and tie." *The Cattleman*, Vol. 34, pp. 31-32, 96-100 (January 1948).

Pound, Louise, "Old Nebraska folk customs." *Nebraska History*, Vol. 28, pp. 3-31 (1947).

Prentis, Noble L., "Pike of Pike's Peak." Kansas State Historical Society, *Transactions*, Vol. 6, pp. 325-336 (1900).

Raine, William MacLeod, *Famous Sheriffs and Western Outlaws*. New Home Library, New York, 1944.

Raymond, Elvira, Letters, 1842-1843, (Manuscript. University of Oregon Library).

Regur, Dorothy, "In the bicycle era." *Palimpsest*, Vol. 14, pp. 349-362 (1933).

Reid, Elizabeth, *Mayne Reid, a Memoir of His Life*. Ward and Downey, London, 1890.

Reminiscences of Oregon Pioneers. Pendleton, Oregon, 1937.

Richardson, Warren, "History of the first Frontier Days celebrations." *Annals of Wyoming*, Vol. 19, pp. 39-44 (1947).

Richter, Francis C., *Richter's History and Records of Baseball*. F. C. Richter, Philadelphia, 1914.

Rise, Cyrus, "Experiences of a pioneer missionary." Kansas State Historical Society, *Collections*, Vol. 13, pp. 298-318 (1915).

Rister, Carl C., *Oil! Titan of the Southwest*. University of Oklahoma Press, Norman, 1949.

Roberts, T. F., "Pioneer life in western Dakota." *North Dakota History*, Vol. 15, pp. 154-168 (1948).

Roosevelt, Theodore, *The Rough Riders*. P. F. Collier & Son, New York, 1899.

Root, Frank A., *The Overland Stage to California*. Topeka, Kansas, 1901.

Rourke, Constance, *Troupers of the Gold Coast*. Harcourt, Brace, New York, 1928.

Ruede, John, *Sod-house Days, Letters from a Kansas Homesteader, 1877-78*, edited by John Ise. Columbia University Press, New York, 1937.

Sabin, Edwin L., *Kit Carson Days*. A. C. McClurg, Chicago, 1914.

Schmitt, Martin, "Frontier mule power." *The Cattleman*, Vol. 81, p. 36ff. (October 1946).

Schmitt, Martin F., and Brown, Dee. *The Fighting Indians of the West*. Charles Scribner's Sons, New York, 1948.

Scott, Willard, "Associational sermon." Nebraska State Historical Society, *Transactions*, Vol. 3, pp. 230-242 (1892).

Sharp, Mildred J., "Early cabins in Iowa." *Palimpsest*, Vol. 2, pp. 16-29 (1921).

Sheldon, Addison E., *Land Systems and Land Policies in Nebraska*. Lincoln, Nebraska, 1936.

Sheldon, Henry D., Papers. 1903. (Manuscript, University of Oregon Library).

Shepherd, Major W., *Prairie Experiences in Handling Cattle and Sheep*. Orange Judd, New York, 1885.

Shipman, Mrs. O. L., "Letter to Texas State Historical Association." *Southwestern Historical Quarterly*, Vol. 52, p. 237 (1948).

Siringo, Charlie, *A Texas Cow Boy; or, Fifteen Years on the Hurricane Deck of a Spanish Pony*. M. Umbdenstock & Co., Chicago, 1885.

Smith, Henry Nash, *Virgin Land, the American West as Symbol and Myth*. Harvard University Press, Cambridge, 1950.

Smith, Ralph, "The Farmers' Alliance in Texas, 1875-1900." *Southwestern Historical Quarterly*, Vol. 43, pp. 346-369 (1945).

Sonnichsen, C. L., *Roy Bean, Law West of the Pecos*. Macmillan, New York, 1944.

Spring, Agnes Wright, *The Cheyenne and Black Hills Stage and Express Route*. A. H. Clark Co., Glendale, Calif., 1949.

"A steam wagon invented by an early resident of South Dakota." *South Dakota Historical Collections*, Vol. 10, pp. 362-387 (1920).

Steinel, Alvin T., *History of Agriculture in Colorado*. Fort Collins, 1926.

Stoddard, Henry Luther, *Horace Greeley*. G. P. Putnam's Sons, New York, 1946.

Studer, Carl L., "The first rodeo in Texas." *Southwestern Historical Quarterly*, Vol. 48, pp. 370-372 (1945).

Swisher, J. A., "Billy Sunday." *Palimpsest*, Vol. 11, pp. 343-354 (1930).

Taft, Robert, *Artists and Illustrators of the Old West, 1850-1900*. Charles Scribner's Sons, New York, 1953.

———, *Photography and the American Scene*. Macmillan, New York, 1938.

Taft, Robert, "The pictorial record of the Old West, Pt. V." *Kansas Historical Quarterly,* Vol. 16, pp. 113-135 (1948).

Tait, Samuel W., Jr., *The Wildcatters, an Informal History of Oil-Hunting in America.* Princeton University Press, Princeton, 1946.

Talbot, Ethelbert, *My People of the Plains.* Harper & Brothers, New York, 1906.

Taylor, Frank J., and Welty, Earl M., *Black Bonanza.* Whittlesey House, New York, 1950.

Thompson, Roy, "The first Dunker colony of North Dakota." *North Dakota Historical Collections,* Vol. 4, pp. 81-100 (1913).

Tilghman, Zoe A., *Outlaw Days.* Harlow Pub. Co., Oklahoma City, 1926.

Tompkins, Colonel Frank, *Chasing Villa, the Story behind the Story of Pershing's Expedition into Mexico.* Military Service Pub. Co., Harrisburg, 1934.

"Town boomers and their advertising." *Kansas Historical Quarterly,* Vol. 9, pp. 97-99 (1940).

Turnbull, George S., *History of Oregon Newspapers.* Binfords & Mort, Portland, 1939.

Tuttle, Daniel S., "Early history of the Episcopal church in Montana." Historical Society of Montana, *Contributions,* Vol. 5, pp. 289-324 (1904).

Union Pacific Railway, Passenger Department. *The Oregon Short Line Country,* Omaha, 1885.

U. S. Congress, Senate, 21st Congress, 2d. Session. *Executive document 38.*

Van Zant, Henry Clay, Letters, 1838. (Manuscript. Authors' private collection).

Vincent, Henry, *Story of the Commonweal.* W. B. Conkey Co., Chicago, 1894.

Walker, Arthur L., "Recollections of early day mining in Arizona." *Arizona Historical Review,* Vol. 6, pp. 14-43 (April 1935).

Walsh, Richard J., *The Making of Buffalo Bill, a Study in Heroics.* Bobbs-Merrill, Indianapolis, 1928.

Warner, C. A., "Texas and the oil industry." *Southwestern Historical Quarterly,* Vol. 50, pp. 1-24 (1946).

Webb, Walter P., *The Great Plains.* Ginn & Co., Boston, 1931.

Wells, Evelyn, and Peterson, Harry C., *The '49ers.* Doubleday, Garden City, N. Y., 1949.

Wells, Philip F., "Ninety-six years among the Indians of the Northwest—adventures and reminiscences of an Indian scout and interpreter in the Dakotas, as told to Thomas E. Odell." *North Dakota History,* Vol. 15, pp. 265-312 (1948).

Westermeier, Clifford P., "Cowboy capers." *Annals of Wyoming,* Vol. 22, pp. 13-25 (July 1950).

——, *Man, Beast, Dust; the Story of Rodeo.* World Press, Denver, 1947.

White, William Allen, *Autobiography.* Macmillan, New York, 1946.

Wik, Reynold M., *Steam Power on the American Farm.* University of Pennsylvania Press, Philadelphia, 1953.

——, "Steam power on the American farm, 1830-1880." *Agricultural History,* Vol. 25, pp. 181-186 (1951).

Wiest, Edward, *Agricultural Organization in the United States.* University of Kentucky, Lexington, 1923.

Williams, Moses A., Diaries, 1850-1896. (Manuscript. University of Oregon Library).

Willson, C. E., "From variety theater to coffee shoppe." *Arizona Historical Review,* Vol. 6, pp. 2-13 (1935).

Wilson, Bushrod, Letters, 1850-1854. (Manuscript. University of Oregon Library).

Winch, Frank, *Thrilling Lives of Buffalo Bill and Pawnee Bill.* S. L. Parsons, New York, 1911.

Wister, Owen, *The Virginian.* Macmillan, New York, 1902.

Winslow, Charles Frederick, "Nantucket to the Golden Gate in 1849, from letters in the Winslow Collection," transcribed by Helen Irving Oehler. California Historical Society, *Quarterly,* Vol. 29, pp. 1-18, 167-172, 255-260 (1950).

Writers Program, Colorado, *Colorado.* Hastings House, New York, 1943.

Writers Program, Wyoming, *Wyoming.* Oxford University Press, New York, 1941.

Wright, Carl C., "Reading interests in Texas from the 1830's to the Civil War." *Southwestern Historical Quarterly,* Vol. 54, pp. 301-315 (1951).

Wyman, Walker D., "California emigrant letters." California Historical Society, *Quarterly,* Vol. 24, pp. 17-46, 117-138, 235-260, 343-364 (1945).

Young, Hiram H., "A Hoosier in Kansas, diary, 1886-1895," edited by Powell Moore. *Kansas Historical Quarterly,* Vol. 14, pp. 166-212, 297-352, 414-446 (1946).